NEW MILESTONES
Sculpture, Community and the Land

Joanna Morland
for
COMMON GROUND

Published by Common Ground 1988
45 Shelton Street, London WC2H 9HJ

© Common Ground 1988
An Historical Perspective © Richard Cork 1988
All photos © Common Ground except page 6 © Paul
Lipscombe 1987; page 61 © Reg Vincent, Portland 1987; page
65 © John Maine 1987; page 68 © Geoff King, Taunton 1988.

ISBN 1 870364 03 1

Typeset and designed on a desk top computer by Common
Ground at Neals Yard DTP Studio, Covent Garden, London.

Printed by Wincanton Litho, Wincanton, Somerset
on 100% recycled paper - sylvancoat

CONTENTS

ACKNOWLEDGEMENTS

We are indebted to numerous people and organisations for their enthusiasm and support for the New Milestones Project and its work. We would particularly like to thank: Maurice Ash, Sue Bell, Alex Czaky, Tony Foster, John Fowles, Elisabeth Frink, Robert Hutchison, John Hubbard, John Lane and Alistair Warman for their encouragement and valuable comments especially in the formative months of the Project.

We are extremely grateful to the Calouste Gulbenkian Foundation and the Henry Moore Foundation for financial assistance throughout the pilot phase, and to South West Arts and the Chase Charity for grants towards publicity and equipment costs.

The first 'New Milestone' sculpture commissions have been made possible with grants and donations from many organisations and individuals. We are grateful to South West Arts for its generous financial support for each commission. We should also like to thank the following for grants and donations towards individual sculptures : ARC (Southern), Barclays Bank (Taunton), Cerne Valley Parish Council, the Elephant Trust, European Year of the Environment, Portland Town Council, TSW - Television South West, Underhill Community Association, West Dorset District Council, Weymouth and Portland Borough Council and the numerous individuals who have given donations, large and small, in cash or in help, materials and services.

Our thanks go particularly to the commissioners and sculptors who have collaborated with Common Ground to create the first 'New Milestones': Christine Angus, Will and Pam Best, John Bone, the Chesil Gallery, Andy Goldsworthy, John Maine, John and Jenny Makepeace, Peter Randall-Page, Simon Thomas, Wilfrid Weld; to Margaret Leicester and Fred Morris, former Mayors of Portland, and the Mayor, members and Town Clerk of Portland Town Council.

Many people have generously given their time, advice and support to the New Milestones Project and the Officer during the pilot phase and in the preparation of this book. We would especially like to thank: Steve Chettle, Mr Cobb, Rory Coonan, Richard Grasby, Priscilla Houstoun, Caryl Hubbard, Howard Legg, David Nash, Doff Pollard, Barclay Price, Christine Ross, Ian Scott, Roland Tarr, Mr Watkins, Andrew Whittle, and Lesley Greene and Michela Crimmin of Public Art Development Trust.

Finally, we are very grateful for financial assistance from the Henry Moore Foundation, Marks and Spencer and South West Arts which has made possible the publication of this book, and an exhibition and conference to mark the national launch of the Project.

A WORD FROM SOUTH WEST ARTS

Some years ago, when the idea of a pilot New Milestones Project in Dorset was mooted, South West Arts was asked for its response to the idea. We were enthusiastic then and have become more so now that we can see the sculptures in place, and talk with the local residents and communities who have made them possible, and who refer to them with the pride of ownership.

South West Arts has given funds towards all of the sculptures in its region and to some other activities such as publicity and the national launch, of which this book is part. In all cases, we have been the minority funders and one of the most impressive things about Common Ground and the New Milestones Project has been their ability to raise funds from all sources to more than match our input. It is no easy task in a rural county such as Dorset, which presents few opportunities for private sector fund-raising. A cornerstone of their fund-raising has always been that the local community should have made some financial contribution, however modest, to the work of art. The cake stalls, jumble sales, village hall displays, village picnics at the site, and so on, are important in ensuring that people feel comfortable with the artist and the work of art and that they will continue to enjoy and understand the work and pass their knowledge of it on to others.

A part of our support for the New Milestones Project has been our view that Common Ground has evolved an approach to public art which is entirely appropriate for a largely rural region such as the South West. The careful planning and wide consultation involved in selecting the site, identifying key local people and eventually selecting the artist and introducing him/her to the community are very much in tune with our thinking. Too much public art has been of the "hit and run" variety, where the work of art, however excellent, is left isolated after the artist has gone away.

While the pilot project has been in a rural county with little other visual arts provision, the model holds good for urban and suburban areas and small towns. The important thing is the underlying principle of ensuring that a project is well set up and that the needs of all - the site, the local people, and the artist - are well matched. We have been glad to be involved in the development of the idea, and we are fortunate to have the permanent reminders in Dorset.

We hope that other parts of the region and the country will wish to set up their own New Milestones and leave their marks for future generations.

Christine Ross
Visual Arts and Crafts Officer
South West Arts

April 1988

Common Ground is grateful to South West Arts for early and continuing support towards sculpture commissions and the national launch of the New Milestones Project.

WITH THE ASSISTANCE OF

SOUTH WEST ARTS

AN HISTORICAL PERSPECTIVE

For all its timely and refreshing originality, the New Milestones Project can be related to a distinct tradition running through twentieth-century sculpture in Britain. As early as 1910, Jacob Epstein and Eric Gill began planning an immense collaborative venture which would have relied, to a significant degree, on its relationship with the countryside. The two friends, united by their desire to revitalise direct carving and place it at the very centre of their work, hatched an extraordinarily ambitious, not to say visionary plan. They decided to create a sculptural temple in a six-acre stretch of land bordering on Asheham House in Sussex. Gill explained that they wanted to take this unusual initiative because, he wrote, the empty plot seemed to offer them 'the grandest opportunity and it is increasingly evident that it is no use relying on architects and patrons and dealers.' The young sculptors interviewed the owner of Asheham, visited Stonehenge for inspiration and travelled to quarries at both Portland and Wirksworth for suitable stone. In September 1910 Gill reported excitedly that 'Epstein and I have got a great scheme of doing some colossal figures together (as a contribution to the world), a sort of twentieth-century Stonehenge.' He transmitted his enthusiasm to Augustus John, who insisted in a characteristically outspoken letter that 'the Temple must be built. People will take to their heels at the sight of so stupendous a thing walking about in daylight.'

Just how these megalithic images would have related to their envisaged site remains unclear. The pagan temple at Asheham was never realised, and Epstein's only surviving record of its likely appearance is a drawing he inscribed with the title 'One of the Hundred Pillars of the Secret Temple.' Like Gill's uninhibited carving of 'Ecstasy', which can likewise be linked with the scheme, it is dedicated to a frank celebration of erotic delight. The woman whose limbs intertwine so sinuously with her lover suggests that Epstein had been studying the most seductive of Indian carvings. But the sensual, curvilinear style adopted in the pillar itself gives way to a more brusque and angular idiom on the architectural surround. Here the little figures balancing on top of each other show how Epstein's interest in 'the Eygptian rooms and the vast and wonderful collections from Polynesia and Africa' in the British Museum was beginning to bear exotic fruit.

The abandonment of the temple project did not prevent Gill from retaining a keen interest in the possibilities opened up by landscape sites. A year later, when Roger Fry commissioned him to produce a large stone figure for the garden of his home on the outskirts of Guildford, he allowed the prospect of the River Wey and St. Catherine's Hill beyond to affect his statue's form. On the back of the drawing for the garden sculpture, he wrote about the 'jolly fine view' from the place where Fry intended the carving to be placed. 'The statue', emphasized Gill, 'should echo the slope of the hill and "appreciate" the view.' Even though it was intended for a horticultural location, which Fry had designed himself with advice from Gertrude Jekyll, Gill was sufficiently impressed by the distant countryside to aim at a felicitous correspondence between the carving and its rural setting.

In 1938 this line of thinking was taken a great deal further by Henry Moore, after accepting an invitation from the architect Serge Chermayeff to make a sculpture for the grounds of 'Bentley Wood', a house he was building for himself near Halland in Sussex. The place Chermayeff had in mind was located 'at the intersection of terrace and garden', where he thought a standing figure might be installed. But Moore, after visiting the site, thought the low-lying character of both house and surrounding Downs called for a horizontal image instead. He wanted the sculpture to be in harmony with the countryside rather than contrasting with it. Since the principal thrust of his development during the 1930s had been directed towards an ever more integral relationship between the female figure and the earth on which she rests, the Chermayeff venture provided him with an ideal opportunity to take this obsessive fusion one stage further.

Until then, he had worked on the central metaphor of woman-as-landscape with no knowledge of his work's destination, and the completed carvings often lingered in his studio for many years before they found a purchaser. Now, however, he knew from the outset precisely where the 'Recumbent Figure' would lie, and the Sussex countryside had an important effect on the form it assumed. The cavity he made within the stone had a unprecedented largeness of conception, surely inspired by the 'great sweep of the Downs' which Moore found so impressive at Halland. The knowledge that 'Recumbent Figure' would come to rest in a place dominated by a landscape he admired very deeply was bound to nourish his conception of the work. It exudes a sense of imperturbable assurance which must likewise have been indebted, in part at least, to the location Chermayeff provided. The setting also stimulated Moore to bestow on the figure's head a more noble and far-seeing vigilance than the almost featureless Wakefield carving he possessed. Looking out over the Sussex hills made him determined to ensure that 'her gaze gathered in the horizon', and the omniscient expression he gave 'Recumbent Figure' would recur in many of the outdoor works he went on to create in later years.

None of them, though, was produced for rural locations as sequestered as the sites chosen by the New Milestones Project. Although some of Moore's post-war works have been photographed in the remote Scottish moorland estate of Glenkiln, they were only placed there after their owner, W.J. Keswick, acquired them from the sculptor. Most of Moore's post-war bronzes were produced within the contained context of the grounds surrounding his studio-home at Much Hadham. And in the most memorable recent attempt by British artists to fuse their work with a landscape setting, Ian Hamilton Finlay and his wife Sue set about making a garden of their own at Stonypath. In this extensive marriage of sculpture and horticulture, which has grown steadily since 1967, the Finlays attain a notably sensitive balance between art and nature. Carved inscriptions to admired painters of the past occupy carefully judged positions within areas of the landscape planted in homage to the work they produced. At every step, object lessons are offered in how to integrate sculpture with the earth it inhabits. Fronting the Finlay's house an English garden contains a profusion of flowers, a walk paved by slabs bearing the names of types of sailing vessels, and a sunken garden harbouring a one-word poem on a weather-worn stone. But as we walk round the house towards the out-buildings, the scale changes from intimacy to grandeur. Against an epic backdrop of the Pentland Hills a small loch appears, created by the Finlays when they dammed a tiny stream, and on the water are glass fishing-floats inscribed with poems. Literature is as important as sculpture in Finlay's work, especially within the Garden Temple where the heart of Stonypath's meaning is located. Inside the building a spirit of stern dedication soon becomes apparent, with carvings on plinths extolling the neo-classical spirit of Saint-Just and the French Revolution.

To move from such a carefully orchestrated site into the countryside itself could easily become a presumptuous enterprise. Many rural locations are cherished precisely because they appear unaffected by human intervention of any kind. The threat of sculptural intrusion becomes even greater when the area is as superlative as Dorset, where the gaunt yet lovely landscape is honoured for its sense of an unbroken link with primordial origins. Reminders of Dorset's prehistoric identity abound; and since the country already boasts a remarkable array of stone crosses, obelisks and standing stones, the New Milestones Project centred on reviving this tradition in contemporary terms. A proper awareness of the past does not, mercifully, allow degeneration into pseudo-archaic excursions. All the sculptors participating in the venture have resisted the temptation to ape spectacular precedents like the White Horse at Weymouth. The new works belong firmly within their own time, and Peter Randall-Page felt that it would be quite inappropriate for him to produce an image large enough to vie with epic chalk drawings in the hillside. Rather than attempting to compete with the grandeur of the clifftop walk from Lulworth Cove to Ringstead Bay, where the bare land continually gives way to the immensity of the water beyond, he opted for a wholly different course. Deciding that anything on a massive scale would be defeated by the sheer vastness of the area, he produced carvings of relatively modest dimensions instead. It was a well-judged conclusion to reach. Walking up the clifftop, we find our eyes falling with pleasure on the fossil-like forms, each one nestling within a dry stone niche set into the grassy bank. These enclosures reinforce the feeling of intimate encounter which the sculptor wanted to engender. But the carvings still relate very closely to the surrounding country. Their shapes pay implicit tribute to the richness of fossils in this part of the Dorset coast, as well as echoing the ample yet tightly curved rhythms of the hills around the niches.

In total contrast to the wayside-shrine aspect of Randall-Page's work, Simon Thomas elected to place his sculpture out on exposed grass nearby. No enfolding walls protect his four wood carvings from the elements. Inspired by Thomas's discovery that part of the land was devoted to grain cropping in the Bronze Age, their forms evoke the germinating power of the grain itself. Just as Randall-Page had used a hard local limestone for his contribution, so Thomas hewed the quartet of carvings from an ancient oak tree which had fallen on the Weld estate a quarter of a century before. The choice of such a weather-worn material helps to integrate these images of fertility with the earth they inhabit. Lying like four swollen mouths between the centuries-old grain land and the present-day wheat and barley fields, they seem determined to broadcast the delights of ripeness to the four corners of this austere yet beguiling landscape.

In common with Randall-Page and Thomas, Andy Goldsworthy concluded that the Working Woodland site at Hooke Park demanded 'something smaller' than the tree-filled area around his sculpture. But he finally produced two sizable rings on either side of the road at the woodland entrance. Part of the time they act as a barrier to cars, and the sculpture is then at its least resolved. While the two projecting 'arms' fulfil their role efficiently

New Milestones

enough, they dissipate the coiled energy contained in Goldsworthy's circular clusters of bent pine. When the 'arms' are raised, and restored to the clusters, they ensure that the work as a whole is charged with tension. It calls to mind Ezra Pound's remark about his celebrated marble portrait by Henri Gaudier-Brzeska. Recalling that the hieratic 'Head' 'was most striking, perhaps, two weeks before it was finished', Pound declared that 'there was in the marble a titanic energy, it was like a great stubby catapult, the two masses bent for a blow.' Goldsworthy's bound pine exudes a similar vitality, but the two clusters also seem to proffer an invitation. Aimed at the scale of a walker or rider, they draw onlookers forward, enticing them to penetrate the mysterious darkness of the wood beyond the road.

Goldsworthy's sculpture has already established itself as a local landmark, and Christine Angus's carving will probably perform a related function when she completes it later this summer. Positioned at the meeting place of five paths, it stands on a hilltop which demands that the work acts as a beacon-like monument identifying the eminence it occupies. Angus is eager to make the work fulfil those expectations, and she sees the large vertical stone in the foreground of her triangular site as a marker. But its interlocking structure is also redolent of interdependence - a theme she considers central to the philosophy behind the Manor Farm whose owners commissioned the sculpture. Since they recently adopted a more organic approach to their work, Angus responded by making all her carvings embody the interaction between delicately balanced natural forces. The planting of twenty-three beech and wild cherry trees will eventually transform the sculpture, and Angus is taking their future appearance into account as she continues working there.

The most epic of all the New Milestones works so far is, without doubt, John Maine's ambitious project at Chiswell. Intended to commemorate the completion of the sea defence system at the village, it will rise in undulating terraces from the coast path. Maine wants each stone wall to evoke the motion of the waves, whose action has exerted such a powerful eroding force at the Portland end of Chesil beach. But between the terraces earth platforms will be created and planted with local grasses, thereby symbolising the regeneration of Chiswell. The scale of the surroundings poses a particular challenge to Maine. He will need to acknowledge its grandeur without imposing on the site a sculpture that violates its allotted space and provokes understandable resentment among people required to accept it as a permanent part of their surroundings. Any evaluation will have to await its completion, but Maine's drawings indicate that he made every attempt to arrive at a thoughtful marriage between image and setting. In this respect, it is fully attuned to the spirit behind the entire New Milestones Project - an initiative dedicated to proving that good sculpture, alive to the demands of the places it enlivens, can become an indispensable part of life.

Richard Cork
April 1988

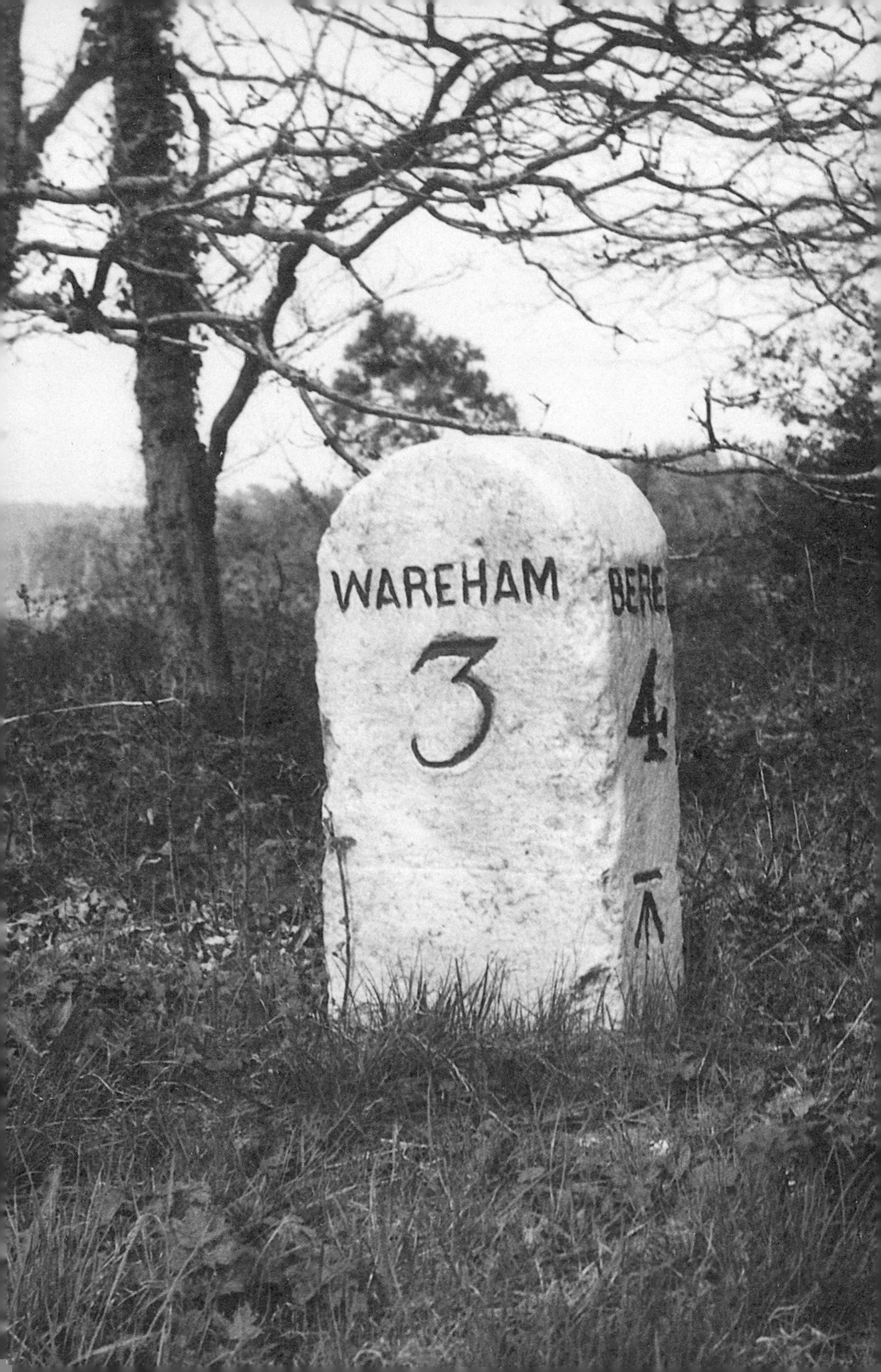
WAREHAM
3
BERE
4

PUTTING THE NEW MILESTONES PROJECT IN ITS PLACE

The New Milestones Project is about what places mean to the people who live in them, about how to express that meaning in an imaginative and accessible way through sculpture.

In encouraging people - landholders or local communities - to commission craftspeople and sculptors to crystallise feelings about their place in a public and permanent way, we are not only trying to liberate sculpture into the wild and to give anyone courage to commission art, however modest, to help communicate their caring. We are emphasising that our feelings about our everyday landscapes are important and should be taken seriously, that our moment in history has something to offer and that in setting our imagination free to explore place we can help initiate new cultural touchstones worthy of our time.

It is a fond imagining of city-dwellers that the country remains static, fossilized in a constant state of bucolic privilege, that anything that is green is 'natural' and that the landscape is a simple unchanging backcloth. These are falsehoods, but perhaps the myths persist because of a deep need within us for consistency and permanence in the countryside when everything around us is changing so fast.

The city, it has been said, is humankind's greatest artistic act. We believe it self-evident that in England (perhaps in Britain) the country-side is our greater if more subtle creation. Thousands of years of hard work in the land and cultural understanding of it are echoed in the landscape we have built. Every piece of land is unique; the rocks, the form of the land, the place where it is, the production processes it has supported - agricultural, mining, building; the investment it represents and receives; its ownership and the rights over it; the social relationships it encourages;

New Milestones

the politics it sustains - all are apparent in the landscape. Almost every corner has been made by our activities. The geology and topography, of course, dominate, but the fine grain of the landscape has been socially constructed. Every piece of land, even the wildest moor, expresses not just the present uses, but past activities and relationships. Like old documents, paintings, literature, buildings and dialect, the land holds many keys to an understanding of our past, our present and particularly the evolution of our common culture.

Thousands of years of human activity have enriched the variety in the landscape, and generation after generation have built meaning into their places of living, work and play. It is only within the last four decades that we have extended our technical capacities and economic rapaciousness to change the land for all time. Deep ploughing obliterates subtle ancient field patterns, complex heavy machinery can remove miles of hedge and acres of ancient woodland in a week. Bulldozers can raze stonewalls and buildings to the ground and fill in marshland. Fertilizers encourage coarse grasses and cereal growth and the competition smothers wildflowers. With them (assisted by pesticides and pollution) the butterflies and bees, the small mammals and birds all disappear. Footpaths, commons and wild wood are lost as farming, industry, commerce, transport, and housing become ever more greedy for land.

The rape of the British countryside in less than half a century has been catastrophic for people, wild life, for cultural diversity and historic continuity.

In 'Tongues in Trees ' (in press) Kim Taplin says *the erosion of the countryside also means a dwindling of the stock of proper food for the imagination and the spirit.*

What does this mean to people, to our humanity and our identity? What does an individual feel when access to the land is measurably more difficult, and less rewarding an experience when he or she gets there? How do our artists, poets, composers feel about a major source of their creative inspiration being so eroded?

There are many reasons for the low level of concern: a deep-seated indoctrination that we must produce food at any cost because of our World War Two experience; the continued propaganda that all farmers are natural "custodians" of the countryside; increasing mobility of people and a lack of knowledge or memory about how diverse and rich our land was only half a lifetime ago.

The New Milestones Project may seem a very small measure in relation to the enormity of the problems facing the countryside; it may seem an oblique idea. It will take hundreds of policy changes, incentive schemes and changed attitudes to make the countryside better for people, wild life and domesticated animals.

New Milestones

But what is needed is imagination and humanity, and from scattered small beginnings Common Ground feels it is vitally important to celebrate what remains, to become more aware of what our surroundings mean to us, as a starting point for local action.

Why Dorset was chosen for the pilot phase of the Project

The original idea was for two 'pilot' areas - Yorkshire and Dorset - two counties with diverse landscapes with definite identities and continuing stoneworking industries, so we could learn and compare results in two very different places.

As it happened we only raised enough funding to work in one place and we chose Dorset for very personal reasons. One of us, Angela King, lives in Dorset and has a special attachment to the place. Having walked all the rivers, working to protect the otter, and having researched much of its species and habitat diversity, she knows the land intimately.

The history and prehistory of the landscape of Dorset is still very apparent - the strip lynchets, barrows, hilltop forts, sunken lanes, drovers' roads are etched into it - and we were drawn to the cultural continuity they reveal.

The landscape speaks of ancient people, but also of Paul Nash, William Barnes and Thomas Hardy. It brings us great joy that John Fowles and Elisabeth Frink live in Dorset, and that they too have already left their distinctive marks on the place.

It has to be admitted that if the project had started elsewhere, our enthusiasm and commitment for it would not have been as great!

These are the advantages. There were considerable disadvantages in the choice of Dorset as a starting point which we discovered by degrees. There is no arts officer for Dorset (although an arts development officer has just joined Dorset Community Council) and Dorset as a county puts little money into the visual arts. The rate base in Dorset is very low - there is very little industry - oil exploitation started this decade. Dorset is conservative with a big and small C. There is no city or large centre of learning. The cultural activities are scattered. It is on the edge of the regions of the regional tourist board, regional arts association, TVS/TSW, and has arguably received less attention than counties which lie in the middle of their ranges.

Art for People and Places

Public art has generally been commissioned by wealthy individuals, large companies, or large public bodies almost always in cities. Often ideas have focused around 'spaces and sites' not places, around 'the public' not people - abstractions which allow arrogance in commissioner and artist.

Rarely has a community, especially in a rural area, thought itself capable of commissioning a craftsperson or artist. War memorials are the exception and a sad one. Why should sculpture be confined to large towns and cities? Is the countryside to be forever regarded as a cultural desert? It is thought by some that outdoor sculpture is an intrusion, whereas the destruction of the countryside and reduction of diversity is not!

Our hope is that the New Milestones Project is one of many measures which will rekindle an interest in local distinctiveness and be at the start of a balanced city/country renaissance with humanity and imagination at its centre.

Sue Clifford and Angela King, Common Ground

New Milestones

COMMON GROUND

The New Milestones Project is one part of the work of Common Ground, a small national charity which was established in 1983. Common Ground is concerned with the conservation of nature and landscapes, focussing on the ordinary and commonplace features which people have around them and are close to in their everyday lives. Without denying the importance to our collective consciousness of nationally recognised buildings, landscapes and historical sites, rare and threatened species of plants and animals, Common Ground is setting alongside these the importance of the familiar and shared experiences in our daily social and cultural life.

JOHN FOWLES has written that collecting things, chasing the rare, and labelling as special:

drains nature of its complexity, of its richness, of its poetries, of its symbolisms and correspondences, of its power to arouse human emotions - of all its potential centrality in human existence.....

What he is saying is that this scientific approach to nature, (which also could include towns, cities - places), somehow devalues familiar places and things and our personal attachments to them; that overlooking the commonplace and ordinary diminishes a broad and rich cultural experience.

Recognising the arts as a potent means of expression, of crystallising thought and strengthening resolve, Common Ground is involving artists from all disciplines to help explore the imaginative, emotional and cultural aspects of our relationships with the world about us. The aim is to encourage people to look afresh at their surroundings, to express and share with others their feelings for the local things which are important to them, to unlock their love for their place. Alongside this, Common Ground is also publishing and promoting practical information on ways in which people can care for their locality and the things in it which they value.

The three major projects of Common Ground - the Parish Maps Project; Trees, Woods and the Green Man and the New Milestones Project - share the same philosophy, each approaching it from a slightly different angle. The Parish Maps Project encourages local communities to create a 'map' of their self-defined neighbourhood showing the features and places which people care about, and to put the map in a public place. Trees, Woods and the Green Man is exploring the cultural, aesthetic and historical significance of trees, inviting participation across the wide spectrum of artforms in the celebration of trees and woods, and promoting practical action. The New Milestones Project is encouraging a new generation of permanent sculptures in towns, villages and the countryside - works which grow from and enrich local places.

Common Ground is attempting to broaden the base of conservation so that it becomes the concern of us all, not just that of experts from a few disciplines and specialisms. In our work we are constantly striving to reach new ears, eyes and minds through publications, postcards, broadsheets, exhibitions, events, articles in diverse magazines and periodicals. Common Ground aims to act as a catalyst, fostering new collaborations between arts, environmental and community organisations; encouraging the authorities and decision-makers to value local opinion and local diversity; giving people courage to share their love for their place, to speak out when insensitive changes are proposed and to turn their passive interest into active, practical caring.

THE NEW MILESTONES PROJECT

The aim of the Project is to encourage and assist Parish Councils, local groups and individuals to commission sculptures or craftwork which celebrate and draw attention to an aspect of their place - its history, geology, topography, natural history, people and stories. The idea is that these works should be permanent, making links between the past and present life in a village or neighbourhood, and proposing aspirations for its future. They must have meaning for present-day inhabitants and for future generations, and become a part of the life of the community.

Sculptors and craftspeople are invited to collaborate closely with local people to discuss and decide the theme and location for the work together. Artists are not encouraged to arrive with a ready-formed idea or to make a work without reference to the people or the place. Local people are a rich seam of knowledge, experience and feeling about their place - our aim is to weld this expertise with the creativity, vision and practical ability of the artist. The interpretation of the chosen subject matter is, however, left to the artist. Wherever possible, artists are asked to work in the place, where the work can be seen evolving, and the process of discussion and consultation between artist and commissioners can continue. The emphasis is on sympathetic, often local, materials, and reference to local methods and traditions where appropriate.

Local commissions of this kind are particularly demanding for artists and craftspeople, requiring not only aesthetic and practical skills, but a wish to consult closely with local people, and an ability to give visible, resonant form to spoken thoughts and the often unacknowledged emotions behind them. Common Ground is compiling an index of artists and craftspeople with the needs and constraints of the Project in mind, assisted by an advisory group of well respected artists and administrators. The sculptors for the first' New Milestones' have been drawn from this index.

The name New Milestones is used metaphorically - in telling the distance to two or more places, milestones pinpoint their own location very precisely. They are small, often beautiful, frequently made from local stone, and carry a wealth of history and character in their shape, letterform and style. In the same way, Common Ground hopes that the 'New Milestones' sculptures will be rooted in and speak of their place. It is not intended, however, that they should necessarily have a waymarking function, nor that they should be replicas of old milestones. Instead it is hoped that they will be as evocative of our times as milestones, stone crosses and other landmarks were for our predecessors - artefacts which continue to enrich our lives now.

The sculptures should be accessible to the whole community: beside a footpath or lane, on the village green or in a place which local people particularly value.

New Milestones

Less prominent locations are often preferable, where the work can be encountered casually or in thoughtful mood. Rather than sculptures which dominate their surroundings, either in scale or presence, Common Ground is keen to encourage small-scale imaginative works which complement and conspire with the place, stimulating people to take a fresh look around them - works which will continue to provoke thought and provide renewal. We are acutely aware also of the responsibility the New Milestones Project has to encourage sensitive work which will enhance our countryside and towns. To provoke a rash of permanent works which have neither lasting quality nor the involvement and support of local people would be arrogant and, indeed, could be counterproductive in encouraging care and practical conservation at the local level.

The Project was set up in Dorset as a three year pilot study in 1985, and since 1986 a full-time Project Officer has been based in the county to promote the idea, to liaise with artists and craftspeople and to assist and advise local commissioners with fundraising, artist selection, and practical and legal aspects of the process. Financial assistance throughout the pilot phase has been given by the Calouste Gulbenkian Foundation and the Henry Moore Foundation. South West Arts has given financial support for each of the commissions and for the New Milestones Project leaflet, and the Chase Charity has given a grant for office and photographic equipment.

During the pilot phase four sculptures have been completed in Dorset, and two more are in progress, one of them in Somerset. These have been commissioned by a variety of people: farmers, a major landholder, a hotelier, an independent Trust, and a local art gallery and a Town Council - in each case inviting the participation of a wider group of local people. They stand in different types of setting: woodland, coast, hilltop, river valley and open downland. Experimental work has also been taking place in Lincolnshire and Cleveland to explore how Common Ground can collaborate effectively with local and county organisations elsewhere.

This publication is both a manifesto of the evolving philosophy of the New Milestones Project and the documentation of its work during the   pilot phase. The chapters in Part I describe in detail the six New Milestones commissions, highlighting the pleasures and pitfalls of each. Part II presents in note form much of the information we have gathered, to help others to take forward the idea and benefit from our experiences

Joanna Morland
New Milestones Project Officer

May 1988

For my father, Joe Morland
who loved rivers and green places

Waterrow
RIVERSIDE SCULPTURES
at Hurstone Farm
ST 056252

Hooke Park
ENTRANCE +
Andy Goldsworthy
SY 527999

Godmanstone
+ **TURNING POINT**
Christine Angus
SY 655977

WAYSIDE CARVINGS
Peter Randall Page
SY 784811

++ W. Lulworth

GRAINS OF WHEAT
Simon Thomas
SY 793810

Chiswell

CHISWELL EARTHWORKS +
John Maine
SY 684732

N

NEW MILESTONES in DORSE
COMMON GROUN

PART I

NEW MILESTONES: STORIES OF SCULPTURES

The stories of the first six commissions are related in this section. We have attempted to highlight the pleasures, problems and resolutions of each commission - some unique to a single project, some common to all.

WAYSIDE CARVINGS

The first time I made the spectacular walk from Lulworth Cove to Ringstead Bay, I felt quite overwhelmed both by the beauty of the place and by the sheer scale of the landscape. Initially I found the prospect of making sculpture on the walk quite daunting. The enormous vistas of open downland under cultivation, the spectacular cliffs, the sea and distant horizon seemed impossible to compete with. I realised on that first visit that whatever I decided to make had to operate on a scale which removed it from direct comparison with the scale of the landscape and that anything too assertive which marred the purity of the place would, as well as seeming rather arrogant, be doomed to insignificance and failure in the face of such elemental expanses.

One feels very small in such places and I wanted to make work which would relate to the intimacy of human scale - something on which to refocus the senses before returning to the enormity of land, sea and sky.

My objective which ran parallel with this was to make something which would strike up a resonance with the surrounding landscape by making a distillation of certain aspects of it. This area of the Dorset coast is famous for its abundance of fossils - in fact the chalk cliffs beneath this downland are literally made up of tiny fossils and the nearby Purbeck limestone comprises the fossilised remains of the gastropods, bivalves and ammonites etc which once lived in an ancient sea. I liked the idea of making a kind of tribute to the ancient lives which now constitute our terra firma. I also wanted to incorporate something of the rhythms of the hills into the work - sweeping in broad rounded curves, tightening and plunging into deep gullies.

These were Peter Randall-Page's reactions to the Dorset coast near West Lulworth when he visited the Weld Estate to discuss the first commission of the New Milestones Project.

Common Ground had written to Wilfrid Weld, owner of the 12,500 acre Weld Estate at East Lulworth, on the advice of Sue Bell of the Country Landowners' Association. The Weld Estate

New Milestones

had commissioned a major landscape survey* in collaboration with the County Archaeologist and Landscape Architect. The study considered archaeology, history and ecology, and was intended to *identify those parts of the Estate which have historical interest and to advise on their future management.* Landscape research of this sort, which draws together many disciplines, is rare and is in the vanguard of landscape analysis and estate management. Wilfrid Weld also expressed a positive wish to encourage visitors to explore beyond the well known parts of Lulworth and discover a wider area of the Dorset coast. Common Ground was excited by these twin initiatives, and approached Wilfrid Weld to participate in the New Milestones Project.

The Weld Estate, one of the largest in Dorset, includes two much visited beauty spots, Lulworth Cove and Durdle Door, as well as a 5 mile stretch of Dorset Heritage Coast Path along the stunning coastal downlands. There is also a caravan site, run by the Estate, above Durdle Door. With a vast influx of visitors to contend with during the summer months, many of them on day outings, Wilfrid Weld felt that the rest of the Estate land had much to offer to walkers and holidaymakers, particularly along the coastal strip, but that its qualities were not widely known. He had therefore identified a circular walk of approximately 2 hours from Durdle Door, (or from Lulworth Cove for a more lengthy route), taking in part of the Coast Path along the cliffs and using a higher bridleway to return. The Estate was planning to produce a leaflet showing the route of the walk and points of interest concerning the wild life, geology and archaeology along the way. Common Ground's approach with the idea of commissioning a sculptor to make a work for a place along the path dovetailed neatly with the Estate's concerns and attracted Wilfrid Weld, offering a feeling of going to see something else.

*

Historic Landscape of Weld - the Weld Estate, Dorset, edited by Laurence Keen and Ann Carreck. (Lulworth Heritage Ltd. 1987)

Common Ground undertook to look for suitable artists and consulted the Index of Artists at the Arts Council of Great Britain and South West Arts and talked with many artists and arts administrators. Of the artists put forward, Peter Randall-Page was selected. Common Ground was also in touch with the postgraduate Landscape Sculpture course at the Royal College of Art, and suggested that Wilfrid Weld might also consider offering students the chance to work in this way, to which he readily agreed. Simon Thomas, a young artist from the South West was excited to accept the opportunity.

The Weld Estate agreed to provide a cottage for the two artists for about three months, a wage and materials for the student sculptor, and transport, assistance in kind and materials from the Estate's maintenance section. Common Ground agreed to raise matching money by approaching South West Arts which had already given considerable encouragement during the formative stages of the New Milestones Project, and had indicated a will-

New Milestones

ingness to consider applications for grant support towards suitable commissions.

Peter Randall-Page and Simon Thomas were based consecutively at East Lulworth throughout the late summer and autumn of 1985, and the sculptures were completed and placed along the bridleway in June the following year. An excellent relationship with Chris Rothwell, the estate manager, proved invaluable for Common Ground and the sculptors, who also made friends with their neighbours at the cottage, tenants and workers on the Estate who took a keen and increasingly supportive interest in the evolution of the sculptures.

After an initial visit to the Weld Estate in June 1985 to meet Wilfrid Weld, and to discuss the commission and walk the circular path, Peter arrived in October to begin work:

I decided to make three carvings in Purbeck marble - not a true marble but a very hard local limestone, blue in colour and itself consisting entirely of tiny fossilised gastropod shells. Much prized by mediaeval carvers, Purbeck marble adorns many of our churches and cathedrals in the form of columns, foliage, fonts and other details of special importance. I have always thought Purbeck marble to be one of the most beautiful native stones we have in this country and I felt that the look of preciousness that this material has would enhance the sense of intimacy I wanted to achieve. In the event I found that Purbeck marble is no longer quarried but was extremely lucky to find a small number of pieces which had been quarried over twenty years ago.

I wanted to find a way of giving my carvings their own intimate space in which to be seen and I thought of using the idea of a traditional niche to achieve this. I found a short stretch of the inland section of the walk where the path follows the boundary bank between two fields and is flanked on one side by a steep grassy bank and on the other by a gently sloping field under cultivation with a low horizon and the sea beyond. Into this bank I decided to build three niches - far enough apart not to be visible one from another but near enough to house a group of highly related carvings.

Having found the right location for the sculptures, one of his first visits was to the tenant, Mr Cobb, who farms that area, to invite his interest and collaboration. While somewhat bemused by the notion of sculpture on a working farm, Mr Cobb agreed to the works being recessed into a boundary bank alongside one of his fields where they would not interfere with cultivation, be damaged by the farm machinery or pose a threat to grazing animals.

The carvings were made in a shed behind the cottage in East Lulworth where lifting gear could easily be used to move the heavy stone, and which provided some protection from the weather. The three shell forms were finished by early winter and two of the alcoves were completed with the carvings fixed in place before the winter weather forced work to stop for the year. The third alcove remained half built and was completed in June 1986.

New Milestones

The retaining walls were built of local Purbeck stone using dry-stone walling techniques into which small chambers were built to accommodate each individual carving. For this part of the work I collaborated with Charles Brentnall, a craftsman builder skilled in dry-stone walling, who carried out the main part of the walling to my specification. Formally, this way of presenting sculpture is that of the traditional wayside shrine found in many parts of Europe and Asia - in fact almost all sculpture was made to be seen in niches of one sort or another up until the Renaissance.

The walk is well used even in October and November, when we were working there, and I was much encouraged by the positive responses we received from passers-by. For myself, I found this project both challenging and invigorating. It is in many ways the sort of commission brief I have always hoped for and the combination of the environment and the help and encouragement offered me by the Weld Estate made this something approaching an ideal working situation.

An unexpected and delightful by-product of the Wayside Carvings was the appearance of bright splashes of colourful wild flowers amongst the grass around the sculptures the following spring. Digging into the soil to recess the alcoves had brought dormant seeds to the surface to germinate and flower amongst the coarse grass and thorn bushes, singing the sculptures' presence.

The Wayside Carvings and Grains of Wheat are about a mile from the nearest farm or house, and over two miles from West Lulworth. Gathering responses from local people and passing walkers has therefore been difficult and spasmodic. The bridleway is, however, well used all the year round as Peter noted, with more than 100 people passing on a summer day, and several people using it regularly for jogging, walking and horse riding. It is clear from overheard conversations and chance meetings that the sculptures intrigue and are enjoyed by many people. They have become well known in the Dorset area and are chosen as the particular destination for walks. The Wayside Carvings are included in a booklet of walks in the Purbeck area and marked on one of the route maps as the 'three snails'. The sculptures themselves bear witness to their success as New Milestones - walkers frequently rest or picnic amongst the Grains of Wheat; the Wayside Carvings are becoming polished by the touch of many hands and have bare earth patches in front of them, and offerings of flowers have been found laid on top of the walling alcoves.

Finding... the stone carvings of shells and seeds was a great bonus in providing impetus to a flagging six year old!

GRAINS OF WHEAT

Simon Thomas, a student at the Royal College of Art, arrived in July 1985 to begin making his sculpture for the same circular walk on the Weld Estate. He found himself alone at the cottage in East Lulworth because Peter Randall-Page had injured his elbow and was unable to start work until later in the autumn. Although the two did not meet until the following year, their responses to the coastal downlands were remarkably similar. Simon Thomas says:

The open grandeur of the area called me not to try and contend with it but to make something which was on a human scale, something of an intimate nature within this very open space.

For the first two weeks of his stay, Simon spent time walking the paths, looking at the countryside and thinking. The landscape seemed so immense that he found his attention drawn to the small things close at hand.

Through collecting local seeds both from the hedgerows and also the local grain fields (which created the northern perimeter of the walk), I developed an interest in the historical land use of the area.

To stimulate his thoughts further, he began making a series of hand sized carvings, enlarging small seeds and exploring their form and volume. At the back of his mind was the notion of the coconut which is dispersed by the sea in its covering husk to new fertile areas - perhaps one of these carvings could also be committed to the sea ....

Simon had noted that the bridleway along which the sculptures were to be placed lay between a designated Site of Special Scientific Interest (SSSI) and modern intensively cultivated grainfields. While making the small maquettes, he was shown the large research document on the Estate, 'Historic Landscape of

New Milestones

Weld - the Weld Estate, Dorset', from which he discovered that:

The SSSI land had not been under the plough since the Bronze Age when it was changed from woodland to become one of the earliest recorded sites for grain cropping in Britain. This history of grain cropping in the area excited me, the modified grass grain seemed to symbolise the fertile relationship of men and women and the land.

He decided to make a group of grains of wheat enlarged from his exploratory maquettes to underline the 4000 year history of cultivation in the area. The grains would create a fertility bridge in space and time between the 'Celtic fields' in the area, traces of which are still visible, and the grainfields of today.

During his first few weeks in East Lulworth, Simon had become friendly with his neighbours at the cottage and with some of the estate workers and had shown them his small seed carvings. He had also got to know local people in the village pub in the evenings. Gradually callers began arriving at the cottage to see how he was getting on and discuss the ideas he was working on. One of the things they particularly remarked on was the smooth surface he had achieved on the wooden seeds. Up to this time, Simon had only made 'non-representational' wood carvings, and he made a conscious decision that the large grain sculptures should be easily accessible in terms of craftsmanship, so that people would not be alienated by rough, seemingly badly-made work. Having made the sculpture attractive on this level, he felt that the deeper content could be more readily grasped and accepted.

Simon had been using beech for the small carvings and had decided to use the same wood for his sculpture since it would have been the indigenous species in the area before woodland clearance for cultivation. However the timber which he had earmarked for the carvings turned out to be rotten, beech being a unsuitable wood for outdoor use. The Estate's carpenter, Steve Stevens, suggested a wind blown oak which had fallen some 25 years before. It had seasoned naturally, with a bough holding the trunk away from the ground, and was perfect for carving. A small team of Estate workers were pleased to become involved in the project and helped Simon saw up the trunk into several large sections and transport them to the cottage at East Lulworth. On the enlarged scale, the plump grains he had planned seemed out of scale, so he slimmed them down arriving at a form like an immature wheat seed, or a prehistoric grain.

The four Grains of Wheat were placed on the coastal downlands above Bat's Head in June 1986. They are fixed in place by winged bars screwed to the underside of the sculptures set into cores of concrete with a bulbous base in the chalk. They nestle into the pastureland a few yards from the bridleway, framed by a wide scooped valley with the sea beyond. On the coastal slopes, different coloured grasses reveal traces of rectangular 'Celtic' field boundaries, while in the fields to the north of the bridleway, modern grain production continues.

The field in which the sculptures stand is used by a tenant farmer of the Weld Estate, Mr Watkins, for sheep grazing. The Grains are about the same size and shape as a full grown resting sheep, and when the flock is grouped near the sculptures, the two are almost indistinguishable from a distance. The wooden seeds appear to be much used and enjoyed by the sheep as scratching posts and wind breaks, and the oak has benefited from the quantities of lanolin from the sheep's fleeces which burnishes and protects the wood. A happy co-existence.

ENTRANCE AT HOOKE PARK WOOD

In 1984, Common Ground wrote to John Makepeace, furniture maker and Director of the Parnham Trust, because of his interest in finding new uses for woodlands and for small roundwood thinnings. He proved enthusiastic to collaborate with Common Ground to commission a sculpture to mark the new entrance into the Working Woodland at Hooke Park Wood.

The Working Woodland is a pioneering enterprise to start a School of Woodland Industry where new technologies and designs will be developed for using small roundwood, both in furniture making and in buildings. The project is being established in Hooke Park Wood near Beaminster, West Dorset, where a prototype house with a roundwood structure has already been constructed and a Manpower Services Commission Community Programme Scheme is teaching forestry and woodworking skills to local trainees. It is the initiative of John Makepeace, whose home, workshop and School for Craftsmen in Wood are three miles away at Parnham House.

The idea behind the Working Woodland is to re-establish the economic viability of woodland managed as a renewable resource in the traditional manner. Andy Poore, an experienced forester, and his assistant are introducing additional areas of broadleaved trees into the 330 acres of former Forestry Commission wood. Timber is not clear felled in blocks, but is thinned systematically, producing a continuous supply of roundwood timber and allowing space for trees to mature. The roundwood thinnings, instead of being pulped or burned, will be the raw material on which the products will be based. A public bridleway crosses the wood and the Parnham Trust encourages its use by walkers for pleasure and to see the work which is happening there. This innovative approach brings together an exciting means of developing the potential for future countryside employment and industry, with recreational opportunities and an active awareness of the ecological value of permanent and varied

New Milestones

wild life habitats.

John Makepeace wanted the sculpture at Hooke Park Wood to be a landmark to guide car borne visitors to the wood, and to be expressive of the philosophy of the Working Woodland. Common Ground was interested to reinforce a feeling of welcome to walkers. The artist's brief asked that materials from the wood should be used for the sculpture and that it should incorporate a functional gate to close the drive to cars at certain times.

Andy Goldsworthy was chosen for the commission for his delicate handling and understanding of natural materials, his proven ability to make large permanent works and the philosophical concord between himself, Common Ground and the Working Woodland. He visited Parnham House in November 1985 to meet and talk with John and Jenny Makepeace, before accepting the commission. The weekend was spent discussing the project, and walking in the woods watching forestry work, meeting Andy Poore and becoming attuned to the place.

The hole/arch was my immediate response to the commission - initially taking its curve from the steep banks - a single sunken ring through which cars and people would pass.

The following April, Andy made a longer visit of several days for the filming of a documentary programme for BBC Plymouth's Art Exchange, directed by Howard Perks, and to explore his initial ideas further through a number of sculptural 'drawings' made with branches from the wood. During the months after his first visit he gave much thought to the notion of creating an invitation, a threshold or entrance, and had made drawings of a large arch from roundwood stripped of its bark spanning the track. It became apparent that the engineering problems of making an arch over a 25 - 30 foot span would be daunting.

The site demanded something smaller. The work became two separate rings at either side of the road - on the more intimate scale of the walker or horse rider. I enjoy the seductiveness of a hole which always makes me want to explore the space inside or beyond - a window, opening, invitation, entrance.....

He decided to make the sculpture from trees which had grown with a natural curve to the trunk, philosophically complementing the ideas of the Working Woodland, and finding a use for uneconomic small timber.

I wanted the form to come out of the material and the place. I looked for a material which would mould into the entrance space - in the way that a roadside tree forms an arch.

Andy made drawings of this proposal for the approval of the commissioner and Common Ground, before work on the sculpture could start.

The construction of the Entrance took place over four weeks in July 1986. Andy invited students Samantha Rudd, Lynette Charters, John Ogden and Justin Underhill to work with him on the project, offering them useful experience in making a large permanent sculpture on site. Their help in felling and preparing timber, and building the sculpture was greatly valued. It had been agreed that Andy and the students would be based in the wood. The Parnham Trust would provide them with lunch and supper, as well as access to showers, laundry and drying facilities. A small caravan in the wood, the office for a Community Programme scheme was substituted at the last minute for the promised living space in a hut. The cramped accommodation, with only primitive cooking facilities, had to be cleared of people and belongings by 8.30 every morning. This placed great stress on Andy and the students during a time of hard physical and pressured work, when privacy and a permanent home base were much needed.

Andy found an area in the wood where soil slippage had caused the trees, mainly Douglas fir, to compensate by growing in

natural curves towards the light; and Andy Poore approved their use. Two weeks of labouring work, felling, trimming, sawing and dragging the logs bodily to the forest track followed, to produce enough timber for the rings. The foresters transported the wood to the drive entrance where the bark was manually stripped by Andy and the students to expose the sappy wood beneath.

Each ring was first laid out on the ground as a circle of overlapping trunks, then fixed together with one inch diameter pegs turned out of greenheart in John Makepeace's workshop. The rigid ring was then lifted, (on the first occasion with a tractor grab, on the second with a hand winch anchored to a tree), and pegged to slanting timbers sunk into six foot foundations filled with preserved timber and concrete. Trunks to build up the skeleton rings were selected from the stock of prepared timber and added individually, each being hauled into position with ropes, drilled and pegged securely in at least two places. Further

trunks were chosen and fixed until Andy was satisfied that the right balance and effect had been achieved. During the construction phase, Andy and the students wore hard hats and worked with care, aware that safety procedures were essential to avoid unnecessary risk to anyone in the team.

The 15 foot barriers which operate on the drop bar principle were the final part of the work to be constructed. The slim, gently curving trunks were designed to cross in the centre of the drive, preventing cars entering when the woods are closed, without deterring walkers or obscuring the lure of the woods beyond. When raised, they lift back and disappear into the structure of the rings to complete the sculpture, visible only as longer spars extending above the others. Counterbalances of hollowed logs weighted with molten lead were added in January 1987, after the wood had dried out for several months. Despite their length and weight, the barriers can be easily lifted by one person, fulfilling the functional requirement of the commission brief.

New Milestones

The building of the sculpture was very much a team exercise. The student helpers contributed energy and enthusiasm, despite their uncomfortable quarters and the torrential rain, and the foresters willingly co-operated, giving assistance and advice which greatly eased the project. The usual problems of damaged, broken or inadequate tools and equipment delayed the construction phase, and one in particular caused a great deal of frustration. The pegs for fixing the timber of the rings were not always made to the exact diameter Andy had requested. When too large they could not be driven into the drilled holes through the logs, when too small, the logs could not be fixed securely. Much time was spent chasing drill bits of different sizes to suit the pegs provided, or trying to pare the drill bits themselves.

Young holly bushes have been planted which will grow against the rings softening their junction with the bank, so that the work will become part of the place, not something separate, added and alien. The inner edges of the rings are purposely set at different heights, so that one creates a 3 foot step, while the other rests on the ground with a levelled path beyond enabling walkers with prams, wheelchairs and pushchairs to enter the wood when the barriers are closed.

During 1987, the sculpture was treated with preservative, masking the original golden colour of the wood and setting the rings back visually into the wood. Their shape makes them distinct from the trees behind, the curving timber contrasting with the vertical growth of the living wood.

I have left a touch in a landscape steeped in associations between people and land. It is a social landmark - a passing through place that gives a sense of entering without blocking the way - an invitation. It is a signpost, gateway, boundary marker and milestone that celebrates the beginning of the wood, a landmark by which people give directions - "Go right at the wooden rings".

The Entrance has already become a landmark locally and for

visitors to the Working Woodland; Andy was delighted on a subsequent visit to be accosted by a lorry driver asking the way, who showed him a scribbled map with 'The 2 Rings' shown as a waymark for finding his route.

TURNING POINT AT MANOR FARM

Will and Pam Best of Manor Farm, Godmanstone were contacted by Common Ground in summer 1986 after they had been mentioned by several people as being concerned for ecology in their farming activities and possibly sympathetic to the aims of the New Milestones Project. It was harvest time when that first letter arrived, so it was not until late autumn that they were able to respond. They were intrigued by the idea of commissioning a sculpture for their farm, having already heard of Common Ground's work, and asked to meet for further discussions.

Over the past six years the Bests had been changing from chemical to organic agricultural methods on their farm in the Cerne valley, six miles north west of Dorchester. That first meeting in December 1986 revealed great accord between their wish to work in harmony with natural cycles to cultivate and enrich the land, and Common Ground's own philosophy. They decided to commission a New Milestones sculpture both to demonstrate their support for Common Ground and its conviction that imaginative works, sensitive to their surroundings, can rest quite naturally in and enrich the countryside, and to share their own interest in sculpture with local people.

Will and Pam had already begun to think about suitable places and possible themes for the commission with a number of considerations in mind. The work was to be for the enjoyment of local and casual walkers and those working on the farm and therefore needed to be near one of the public bridleways through the farm. At the same time, it must not be in a position which would interfere with the farm work nor risk damage to the sculpture or farm machinery. It needed to offer a new way of looking at the land yet be firmly rooted in the reality of farming.

The place for the sculpture quite literally emerged in late 1986, when an area of brambles and scrub on the chalk ridge at the western edge of the farm was cleared to plant wild cherry and

New Milestones

beech saplings as part of the County's tree planting scheme. Not only does it have a special quality of calm and seclusion, protected on three sides by mature trees, but when the hedge on the fourth side was laid, it opened up a magnificent vista to the west. This clearing is at the meeting point of five bridleways - including an ancient ridgeway track known locally as the Driftway - a confusing junction for walkers and in need of a distinctive waymark.

The theme was more elusive. Many ideas were put forward to be discussed with the chosen artist who, as a newcomer to the farm and to the clearing, would also bring a fresh approach to the the sculpture's subject matter. Common Ground arranged a slide show of work by sculptors from the New Milestones index of artists and craftspeople, showing a variety of contemporary work in wood, stone and metal. Four artists, all working in stone but making very different kinds of work, were shortlisted. Common Ground sent them each a short description of the farm, its work and surroundings, the site, ideas for themes, and a proposed timescale for the commission, inviting their interest. All replied that they were enthusiastic about the opportunity, and at a meeting on 30 April 1987 between the Bests, Common Ground and South West Arts, it was unanimously agreed to invite Christine Angus to make the sculpture.

Meanwhile, during March and April, the Bests, assisted by Common Ground, had been working to raise funds for the project to add to their own contribution of 3 months accommodation at Manor Farm for Christine, help in kind and some finance. A detailed proposal and a draft budget were drawn up to be used both for grant applications and as a commission brief. By May, two-thirds of the budget had been secured with grants from South West Arts, £1950, and TSW - Television South West, £400. Later, in August, approaches to Cerne Valley Parish Council and West Dorset District Council raised £10 and £100 respectively, and Will Best's brothers, James and Richard, and their families, and a local gallery owner, Elisabeth Bairstow, gave their personal support to the project with donations totalling £800.

Christine made her first visit to Manor Farm in early June. During her two day stay, she had long conversations with the Bests and Common Ground and, with these in mind, explored the farm and village. An important discussion was devoted to practicalities: the budget was examined for vital omissions and to check the adequacy of allocations to each heading, giving Christine a guide to the scale and complexity of work she could contemplate. The proposed timescale and the assistance the farm could offer from its own resources were also touched upon. She went away from Manor Farm with a strong impression of

the recent conversion of the farm to organic methods and the convictions behind this. The impulse of this change and its need was a sensitivity towards and awareness of the balance of nature, the cycles inherent in every aspect, and the interdependence within the whole. The Bests wished to develop a method of working with and being part of a delicately balanced system.

The date for Christine to start work on the sculpture at the farm was in early August. Following her preliminary visit, she agreed to produce drawings of her first ideas for the commission by the end of June, for consideration by the Bests, Common Ground and South West Arts. These contained some of the ideas and themes which had been discussed, but in the short time available, she had not been able to resolve them into a mature proposal. By the agreed starting date, after two more visits for further talks and to select stone in a Purbeck quarry, Christine had arrived at a proposal for a sculpture with three elements placed around the triangular clearing. She says of her proposal:

As the 23 young trees in the clearing develop into a small copse, the feeling and space of the site will change considerably. This meant taking on the element of time and change as a positive aspect of the sculpture.

The three sculptures are not carvings reflecting specific objects; their function is to draw attention to what is happening around them, both physically and in time.

The large piece near the laid hedge is a marker. I decided on its form as a partial consequence of the columns and capitals in the village church. The interlocking form relates to interdependence and interaction. At present this piece is dominating in scale. As the trees grow it will become dwarfed and absorbed into their growth. In turn the stone will mark their growth, verticality and interrelationship.

The sculpture at the rear of the site will be more intimate. Hidden partially by growth and eventually lying under the canopy of trees, I would like it to emphasise that atmosphere peculiar to woods. The sculpture is one stone around another, reflecting another kind of interdependence and interaction.

The third piece will be a written reference to the trees: Beech and wild cherry, the numbers of each, and the date of planting. This will be a continuous point of reference through time to events and changes in the site.

In mid-July, a meeting was arranged at the farm with a district planning officer who advised that planning permission should be sought for the sculpture, and an application was hurriedly submitted in the knowledge that approval could take up to two months. After a slight loss of momentum, it was agreed to go ahead before formal planning permission was granted, bringing the stone into the farmyard instead of taking it straight up to the hilltop. Here Christine could work under cover and near a mains power source while roughing out the two parts of the key element - the column. Seven pieces of Purbeck Portland stone, ranging from 1 to 6 tons were delivered on August 21 and work began. News that planning consent had been granted arrived just over a week later.

News of the Manor Farm sculpture had been filtering out to people in the vicinity through word of mouth and, by late July, with a firm proposal and a starting date, it was time to distribute a leaflet to everyone in the village and to interested people more widely. This was followed soon afterwards by a display at the village fete and an article in the Parish Newsletter, which has proved an excellent means of circulating subsequent progress reports and news. A formal approach was also made to the Parish Council to invite their support for the planning application and to ask for a small donation; the response was positive on both counts.

As a celebration to mark the start of the project, a village picnic was held in the clearing on 27 August 1987. Invitations were delivered to every house, and about 100 people came during the beautiful sunny afternoon and evening to meet Christine Angus, to talk about the sculpture with her and the Bests, and to see the place for themselves. Groaning tables of food had been prepared by the Best family and friends, and £67 in profits and donations was added to the sculpture fund from the event. Donations have continued to arrive from local well-wishers and passing walkers, revealing the enthusiasm aroused by the project and bringing the income up to the budget target of £4,000. A neighbouring farmer

has shown her support in a special way by planting daffodil bulbs in the clearing, remembering the wild daffodils which used to grow there before the area became overgrown with brambles. In time, these cultivated flowers will revert to the wild form more in keeping with the natural plant life of the hilltop.

Christine worked in the farmyard throughout September and October, shaping the two sections of the column and carving them to a close fit where they interlocked. This stage took longer than had been expected, partly due to the sheer volume of stone to be carved, and partly to unexpected problems, causing some tension between the artist and the Bests, who were anxious to reclaim the barn to store their expensive farm machinery under cover.

Eventually on 4 November, the day to move the stones to the clearing arrived. A local lorry owner, Brian Tite, was delighted at the chance to fully test the capabilities of his newly acquired lorry mounted crane. With the lorry on the Driftway, backed tight to the laid hedge, he spent a whole day positioning the column base with Christine and a band of helpers, and patiently raising and lowering the upper section into place, while final adjustments were made to the interlocking faces. As dusk fell, the remaining five stones for the other two elements of the sculpture were unloaded into the clearing. These were moved to their correct positions by another work party organised in late December.

For the next two months, Christine continued carving in the clearing, with a scaffolding and tarpaulin shelter affording some protection from the wind and rain. The column had looked large and intrusive when it was first brought to the site. Several weeks on, it had become part of the place, familiarity with its presence, the softening effect of weathering and the influence of the surroundings upon Christine's subtle adjustments to its shape having all played their part.

At Christmas it was agreed to suspend operations until late March to avoid the worst winter weather and to give both artist and commissioners a break from the pressures of the commission. Christine returned just before Easter to begin work again with renewed energy. She began by refining the column further, slimming it down and, later, adding incised leaf-like shapes to the upper stone. Having painstakingly resolved the principal element, Christine carved and completed the second and third parts in a relatively short time, helped by the longer days and calm, sunny weather. The sculpture was completed at the end of May 1988. The final touch, provided by the Bests, will be a stile to invite walkers in from the Driftway. A natural tunnel through the blackthorn bushes is an enticing entrance from the farm track. The work will undoubtedly acquire a name in time, and this will be cut into the cross bar of the stile to mark the place.

A picnic party has been arranged for Sunday 12 June 1988 when those who have given grants, donations and assistance have been invited to join the Bests and their neighbours from Godman-

New Milestones

stone, Cerne Abbas and beyond, Christine and Common Ground, to celebrate the completion of the commission. On the previous evening, Christine is giving a talk and slideshow about her earlier work and introducing the Manor Farm sculpture.

This commission was the first which the Project Officer was able to follow in detail from start to finish. Will and Pam Best and Christine Angus collaborated closely with the Officer to test ideas and find solutions to problems, and contributed valuable feedback and comments which will inform future projects. We have all learned an enormous amount from the experience: that thorough discussion of the project is essential - to clarify the expectations of both the commissioners and the artist, to identify and find solutions to problems before the project begins, to agree a detailed budget which accurately reflects costs and takes account of the financial implications of the sculpture location, materials and equipment; that agreements and understandings must be confirmed in writing; that both commissioner and artist need privacy and respite from the commission and therefore to share living space results in tension, however much liking there is between the two. The Manor Farm commission undoubtedly had its problems and frustrations, in common with every commission, but the sculpture has been completed and the commissioners and artist have come through the experience by working together and looking for creative alternative solutions.

The sculpture and its development has been the focus of much interest from local people and casual walkers, many of whom visit regularly, often returning with friends, to 'see how it is getting on'. Inevitably there have been a few antagonistic comments; one person remarked: *The only way that will complement nature is when the brambles grow over it again.* But the vast majority of people are enthusiastic and fascinated, and the sculpture is already a waymark for the turning to Manor Farm from the Driftway, as well as being a landmark over a wider area.

I HAD to write and tell you that, walking yesterday, I saw Will Best's sculpture on the hilltop and loved it! It just needs to weather a bit. But that little corner will make a small piece of heaven.

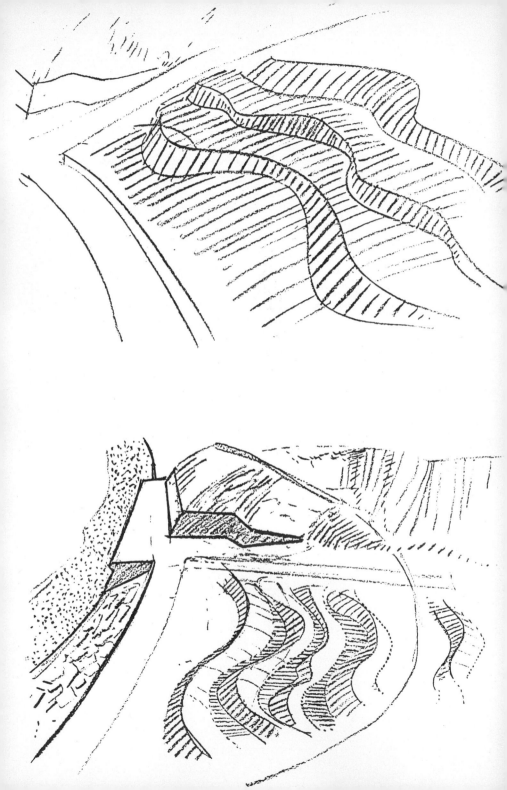

CHISWELL EARTHWORKS

What has now become known as the Chiswell Earthworks started life two years ago, in May 1986, as a plan by the owner of the Chesil Gallery, Margaret Somerville, to offer a sculptor's residency at the Gallery during 1987.

Chiswell, once the largest village on Portland, has been devastated by sea flooding throughout its history. The most recent floods in 1978/79 had so undermined the community that many more inhabitants and businesses moved away from the village. The Chiswell Residents Action Group had been formed to put pressure on Wessex Water Authority and local Councils to tackle the problem of flooding. This successful campaign resulted in a £5.5 million Sea Defence scheme to stabilise and protect the Chesil Beach, to build an interceptor drain to carry flood water away into Portland Harbour and to raise part of the main road to the Island. The scheme was completed in autumn 1986, bringing a guarded optimism about the future security of the village.

In May 1986 Margaret Somerville invited the Consulting Engineers for the Sea Defénces, C H Dobbie and Son, to hold an explanatory exhibition of the Scheme in her Gallery, which stands on the Chesil Beach. It was whilst visiting this exhibition that a local resident suggested a piece of sculpture to celebrate the completion of the Chesil Sea Defence Scheme. In response to this, Margaret planned a three month residency at the Chesil Gallery and approached South West Arts for advice. She was referred to Common Ground as an organisation which could help realise such a project, and the idea of a permanent work for Chiswell, made during a sculptor's residency, took shape.

The artist's brief, drawn up by the Chesil Gallery and Common Ground, suggested that the sculpture should celebrate the completion of the Sea Defences and herald the renewed confidence and revitalisation of the village. The project was originally planned on a modest scale to run for three months, March to May

New Milestones

1987, when the sculptor would be based at the Chesil Gallery, planning and making the commissioned work. An exhibition of drawings and models for the sculpture and a formal unveiling of the permanent work were planned for May 1987. The budget too was modest, amounting to £5,000, including materials, fee and accommodation. Fundraising for this sum began in mid October 1986.

During discussion of who the sculptor should be, John Maine emerged as an obvious choice for a work on Portland. He had already expressed interest in Common Ground's work, and was keen to make a sculpture to remain on Portland, having worked in the quarries there for over 20 years, making sculptures for subsequent siting elsewhere. Through collaborating with Portland masons and quarrymen, he had forged close friendships among the Island's craftsmen and built a great respect for their skills which they reciprocated.

John stayed at the Gallery from December 1986 to May the following year, and while carving another commission, began thinking about a work for Chiswell, talking with local people, reading engineering documents for the Sea Defences and having informal meetings. Slowly ideas for suitable placings for the work, and what it could look like, developed. He isolated three possible locations: in the centre of the village; on the Esplanade; and on West Weares, a rough triangle of grass above the sea wall, at the point where the beach meets the Island.

On 10 April, an evening meeting of local residents was called at the Chesil Gallery through house-to-house leafletting and the local free press. About 10 Chiswell residents and 20 from Portland attended including Skylark Durston, a retired and much respected mason with whom John had frequently worked. Many sketches of ideas for sculpture using stone and the land were displayed on the walls, and John gave a slideshow of his works and his sources of inspiration before opening a general discussion. The debate was lively and constructive, and the general feeling was that a sculpture made especially for the village would attract interest from within and beyond the Island.

A local newspaper reported on the meeting:

This was the chance for opinions to be shared, because no decisions have been made either on the siting or the form that the work should take, although the sculptor has been investigating the possibilities of a West Weares location and his display of numerous proposals of form, which he has produced over the past few weeks, suggest that he favours a work growing out of the site rather than an object taken there.

Many people at the meeting pointed out the instability of the West Weares, but Mr Maine explained that a terraced work could possibly assist in stabilising the land and he said: "It should show that in many cases, art can assist with an engineering problem".

New Milestones

Most of his proposals, all of which appeared to be favourably accepted by the meeting, symbolised Chiswell's distinct role as 'a window to the sea' and featured its association with the quarries.

Some disappointment was expressed that the main street of the village had not been mentioned as a possible site, but the artist and 'Skylark' Durston both expressed the opinion that a work placed there could go largely unnoticed because of the volume of traffic.

"A work away from the centre would encourage people to look at Chiswell as a whole" said John Maine, " and could re-establish the identity of the village and perhaps act as a catalyst for other things to happen".

A second meeting was held on 30 May at St George's Centre, Reforne, Easton, a few miles from Chiswell but more central on the Island, which was attended by Town and Borough councillors, Portland Town Mayor, Borough Engineers, and about 40 Portlanders. John described his evolving proposal for a terraced landscape sculpture on West Weares :

"The proposal takes the form of a landscape work, rising in terraces from the coast path. The curved walls will create wave-like patterns, and support undulating platforms of earth, planted with low-growing species. The higher walls will be made from stone found in the upper strata of the quarries (eg 'Slat'), and lower walls will be constructed from a sequence of different types, in the descending order of stone layers found naturally (such as 'Roach', 'Whitbed' and 'Basebed'). Each type of stone will suggest a different method of wall construction."

The meeting greeted his ideas with enthusiasm establishing a core of local commitment to see the project succeed. The terracing was welcomed as creating stability in an area prone to slippage, as well as creating an amenity where local people and visitors could sit and picnic or watch the sea. Local consultation has continued, even amongst those unable to attend the meetings, through wide press reporting by an interested journalist from Portland, direct contact with the Chesil Gallery, and con-

versations with the sculptor, his many friends and local support-
ers of the project.

Portland Town Council has been closely involved with the
development of the project since John Maine started working on
his proposal and fully supports the Earthworks scheme. The
Council has agreed to accept ownership of the Chiswell Earthworks, including the insurance and maintenance implications,
on behalf of the people of Portland, on its completion. A Trust
Fund to cover future maintenance costs was launched in May
1988 with a donation of £40 from the outgoing Mayor's Fund, and
further local donations and grants will be invited as the work
progresses.

Alongside the meetings with local people, the Chesil Gallery and
Common Ground had been in discussion with local organisations and bodies, those concerned with the landscape and wild
life on the Island, Portland Town Council and with Weymouth
and Portland Borough Council Engineers and Planning Departments. We learned that the whole shoreline of the Island,
including West Weares, had been designated a Site of Special
Scientific Interest by the Nature Conservancy Council. Any
proposal would require the NCC's approval. However, the
Borough Engineers Department informed us that the area identified for the sculpture had been subject to drainage and reclamation works 20 years previously, and that soil from elsewhere had
been brought in to level the area. The Nature Conservancy
Council was therefore delighted that we were proposing to
replace the disturbed soil with Portland soil, and to encourage
indigenous species to the area.

By mid summer 1987 it became clear that an earlier plan to
employ a mason and three apprentices would not provide
enough manpower to construct the work. In July, the Borough
Chief Engineer, Mr Kemble, was invited to discuss the project
with John Maine and Margaret Somerville. He had been responsible for the earlier drainage works on West Weares and was
familiar with the site. It transpired that an unrealised part of that

New Milestones

scheme had been to landscape and terrace the area of West Weares identified for the Chiswell Earthworks. With this revelation of convergent thinking, the Earthworks suddenly became possible. Through Mr Kemble's enthusiastic commitment and intervention, a meeting was immediately arranged with the Borough Council's Manpower Services Management Agency to start the process of setting up a Community Programme team of workers to construct the sculpture, and at the same time repair the faulty land drainage system causing instablity in that part of West Weares.

Developing a scheme proposal and gaining approval from the relevant unions and the MSC Board took eight months. It has however produced important side benefits: a realistic tools and materials budget, a planning application presented to the Borough Council on our behalf, and sound engineering advice. The scheme employing 14 full and part time workers, including a supervisor and a mason foreman starts work in early June, following a 2 week stint of earthmoving and digging by a 30 man Army team. It is hoped that the majority of the earthshaping and wall building work will be completed before the weather breaks in autumn 1988.

I would like to draw together a band of people who know the chosen site well and become sufficiently involved in the spirit of the project to roll up their sleeves and contribute to it John Maine at 10 April Public Meeting.

John Maine, Common Ground and the Chesil Gallery all feel that it is essential to the success of the Earthworks to involve as many local people as possible in creating the sculpture - employing local masons and young trainees; involving students from the Masonry and Carving course at Weymouth College; interesting pupils from the primary school overlooking West Weares in re-seeding and tending the area during its re-instatement; and the Portland Environmental team, based at St George's Centre, in overseeing the re-establishment of indigenous species. Subsequently, contact has also been made with the Borstal on Portland,

and working parties may be able to help. Opportunities will also exist for local sculptors and masons to join in on a voluntary basis.

Having gained local approval for John Maine's terracing proposal, the Chesil Gallery and Common Ground redrafted the budget to cover the firm proposal. Finance for the Chiswell Earthworks has come from: European Year of the Environment, £5,000; South West Arts, £2,750; The Elephant Trust, £750; Weymouth and Portland Borough Council, £500, Dorset County Council, £250; Portland Town Council, £100; Underhill Community Association, £50; and local donations, £100; totalling £9,500. In addition, ARC (Southern), a national quarrying firm and a major employer and stone quarrying concern on the Island, has agreed to give stone for the Earthworks, Portland Plant Hire has offered to give assistance with earthmoving equipment where possible, and the Manpower Services Commission Community Programme has established a 14 person Community Programme team for a year to help construct the Earthworks. In all, these contributions are worth over £80,000.

Although West Weares is an area of open land, it all belongs to someone. The ownership of land on Portland is highly complex, with ancient inheritance customs creating shared ownership of an area by sometimes more than 60 people. Few formal records of ownership exist outside the family, making land owners difficult to trace. Three owners were found for the area of West Weares identified for the sculpture. Weymouth and Portland Borough Council owns a section outright, and Mr Howard Legg and ARC (Southern) have joint ownership of another part. Each was contacted to discuss the Earthworks proposal and the Planning Application for the sculpture. The owners have now each given their formal permission for the sculpture to be built and remain on their land for a minimum of thirty years. By granting permission, they do not lose their rights of ownership, but equally do not own the sculpture itself, nor incur insurance or maintenance liability for it.

New Milestones

The scale of the Chiswell Earthworks sculpture departs from the idea of intimate, small-scale 'New Milestones' which any community can commission. The area of West Weares covered by the terracing will be about half an acre, the longest terraces 54 yards in length. The place chosen for the Earthworks is dominated by West Cliff rising behind to 370 feet, the sea stretching west to the horizon across West Bay, and the extraordinary 20 miles of the Chesil Beach joining the Island to mainland Dorset. John Maine's response to these powerful surroundings has been to design an extensive work which will literally become part of West Weares, drawing attention to the elements which affect Chiswell and its inhabitants, rather than making a carved work which could appear 'out of place' or an unnecessary decoration. The project is more extensive in terms of timescale, finance and size than the other commissions to date and it offers an example to future commissioners to realize more ambitious schemes.

Of a total budget of almost £90,000, less than £10,000 has been raised from grants and donations. The project has been made possible largely through the enthusiasm and support of local industries to contribute their time, materials and assistance in kind, and the willingness of the Manpower Services Commission to provide a Community Programme team to help construct the sculpture. Residents in Chiswell and on Portland, and the Town and Borough Council, have been drawn into the project through careful and detailed consultation during the 18 month planning phase, building on the early support of a handful of councillors and interested local people.

Although interest in the project is widespread on Portland, there have been a few dissenting voices, such as the correspondent to the Dorset Evening Echo who remarked: *Whoever is responsible for suggesting terracing and sculpture at West Weares? It's like applying make-up to a spotty complexion and hoping no one will notice the pimples. First things first, for instance knocking down all those empty dilapidated properties in Chiswell and that appalling derelict garage at Victoria Square. Whoever owns that should be charged with cruelty; it should have been put down years ago. Basics first please, then the frilly bits.* The writer, by putting pen to paper, to some extent substantiates the belief of John Maine and Common Ground that applying thought to one part of the landscape, even if the result is not useful in a practical way, encourages people to look more carefully at their surroundings and to choose the best ways of improving other parts of Chiswell. We hope that the Chiswell Earthworks will both act as a catalyst for future community activity in Chiswell and celebrate the improvements which have already taken place.

RIVERSIDE SCULPTURES AT WATERROW

The first contact between Common Ground and John Bone of Hurstone Farmhouse Hotel, Waterrow, West Somerset, was made by John in November 1986. He had read an article in the Country Landowner, the magazine of the Country Landowners' Association, describing the New Milestones sculptures on the Weld Estate at West Lulworth which re-kindled his own long held wish for a sculpture at Hurstone Farm. It was the first time that publicity about the the New Milestones Project had prompted a potential commissioner to approach Common Ground, and offered us the opportunity to expand beyond the boundaries of Dorset before the official national launch of the Project in 1988.

Hurstone Farm lies beside the River Tone, 9 miles west of Taunton, among dramatic but intimate hills and wooded valleys. It was converted seven years ago to a six bedroom family-run country hotel, reducing and complementing its agricultural activity. Now only 12 acres are farmed by the Bone family to supply the hotel, including a small Jersey herd producing milk for farm-made cheese, a kitchen garden and a recently planted cider orchard. The remainder of the pastureland is let as grazing to neighbouring farmers and 13 acres of established broadleaf woodland are managed by the farm with advice from the Somerset Farming and Wildlife Advisory Group. The River Tone bounds the farm on its west side and the disused Somerset and Dorset Railway runs through its southern edge. The remains of viaduct piers, designed by Brunel, which carried the track across the river still stand among the trees.

John Bone is an enthusiastic conservationist and is active in promoting the economic vitality of his part of West Somerset by encouraging sympathetic tourism which highlights the natural qualities of the area. Among his ideas to attract visitors to use the hotel as a base for walking holidays, he proposes to open a new permissive path and to clear an overgrown existing footpath

New Milestones

through the woods on the banks of the River Tone. This will add a much needed link in the local footpath network, giving local people and visiting walkers access to the river and enabling them to avoid the busy A361 road. Paths from the hotel will also join up with the new path, creating an hour long circular walk for hotel guests through the farm's orchard, pastures and woodland. The paths will be cleared and stabilised in the spring/summer of 1988 by a Community Programme team provided by Taunton Deane Borough Council's Manpower Services Commission Management Agency.

Common Ground is particularly attracted by John Bone's interest in contemporary art and his desire to see the establishment of a long distance path for local people and visitors along the length of the River Tone, from Clatworthy Reservoir in the Brendon Hills to its confluence with the River Parrett near Burrowbridge in east Somerset. His initiative in opening a new public path through his land could spur other riverside landholders to clear existing paths or create new ones at other points along the river. The commissioning of a sculpture at Hurstone Farm will draw attention to the facilities he is offering and encourage more people to use the new path.

The farm and its surroundings suggest a variety of themes: the river, the railway, and the woodland, secondary growth in an ancient wooded area, all offer rich histories. The first shortlisting selection for the commission was made in January 1988, without preconceptions as to theme, style or materials, and four sculptors were chosen from the New Milestones index of artists. Of these, David Nash was selected and made a first visit to Waterrow in late July 1987 to discuss the commission with John Bone and Common Ground. He was enthusiastic about the atmosphere of the woodland footpath and particularly excited by the fallen trees which continued to flourish in their horizontal positions, sending up strong branches towards the light and creating natural stiles across the path. With a provisional agreement to carry out the commission in April 1988, David left with several pages of sketches and notes for works to highlight and draw out the spirit of the woods.

David Nash reluctantly withdrew from the commission in early 1988 due to pressure on his time from other commitments. Although naturally disappointed by this, Common Ground and John Bone are now discussing the commission with Michael Fairfax, a young sculptor who works in wood and stone and who has a particular sensitivity and love for woods. The sculptor made a weekend visit to Hurstone Farm in mid-May 1988 and exciting ideas for fences, bridges and stepping stones to carry walkers over boggy patches in the path, and for sculptures to illuminate aspects of the woods and river and their history were discussed. He will return for a fortnight in mid August 1988 to prepare a detailed proposal for the approval of John Bone, Common Ground and South West Arts. If it is acceptable, it is anticipated that he will be in residence at Hurstone Farm for 10 - 12 weeks from October to December 1988 to create a series of works beside the footpath alongside the river.

The commission budget has been reworked with the new sculptor to take account of his particular needs for materials, equipment and other assistance, and remains the same total, £5,200, as originally discussed with David Nash but allocated to different budget headings. £1,000 has been included, as in the earlier budget, to produce documentation, leaflets on the commission for local distribution, and a Walk Guide which is intended to encourage people to use the path and to enjoy the sculptures and the wild life in the valley.

Fundraising for the commission has been in progress since September 1987 and has proved especially intractable. £4,750 has now been firmly promised: South West Arts has again shown its support for the New Milestones Project by promising a grant of £2,500, the Countryside Commission has offered a grant of £1,300 towards materials, labour and a Walk Guide, and the Taunton branch of Barclays Bank has made a donation of £250 to support

New Milestones

a local environmental initiative. Hurstone Farmhouse is itself able to provide accommodation for the sculptor and his family during the commission and has also offered mature oak as material for the sculptures. Grant applications to local Councils and other bodies are still under consideration and discussions with them about their willingness to accept the change of sculptor have taken place.

In November 1987, Common Ground met officers in the Tourism, Leisure and Recreation, and Countryside Sections of Taunton Deane Borough Council to invite their collaboration in developing a long distance River Tone path. They expressed considerable interest in the sculpture commission and the principle of a river path, and offered to help by sending information on the commission and its aims to Parish Councils in the Borough and by distributing the Walk Guides when they are produced. However, a note of warning was sounded on the length of time required to interest and persuade landholders to create new public paths.

The commissioner and Common Ground are hoping to involve residents in Waterrow and Bathealton Parish in the project by distributing a leaflet on the sculptor's ideas and proposals following his visit in August. When the first sculptures appear in the autumn, an evening gathering will be held at Hurstone Farmhouse with a slideshow and talk by the sculptor, providing a chance for people to meet him and discuss the work. It should also raise some profits for the sculpture fund. The Parish Council will be invited to give their formal support to the project, both verbally and with a token donation. Contact has also been made with the local community secondary school in Wiveliscombe, and a talk and slideshow by the sculptor in school, followed by a visit and walk along the riverside path, have been provisionally agreed. We also expect local schools will wish to bring groups of children to see the sculpture being made, and are delighted that the sculptor welcomes such visits.

Although this commission is still at a formative stage, it promises an exciting challenge to the sculptor with the opportunity to make practical artefacts in a privately owned woodland. We intend to circulate information about the path and sculptures in Waterrow and the surrounding area, and to local Parish Councils and appropriate periodicals and magazines, to encourage other landholders in the Taunton area to increase public access to their land. Above all, Common Ground hopes that local and visiting walkers will discover the sculptures as they explore the new path, and that the works will add to their enjoyment of the woods and river, and that ideas for extending paths along the River Tone will in the longer term be realized.

REFLECTIONS

During the three year pilot phase of the New Milestones Project in Dorset, Common Ground has had several objectives:

- to enable ordinary people/groups to commission works
  of art for themselves
- to create cultural touchstones
- to release sculpture from the confines of gallery and sculpture
  park into places where people live, work and play.
- to assist commissions demonstrating aesthetic aspiration and
  models of community involvement.
- to discover pitfalls and problems and to find alternative solutions.
- to create new collaborations between countryside, environmental, art and community organisations.
- to assess the viability of these objectives and ultimately, to
  launch the Project nationally.

The achievements of the first three years are represented by this publication, the completed commissions and those in progress, the experiences of people and organisations who have been closely involved with the New Milestones work, and the responses of those members of the public who have unexpectedly encountered a 'New Milestone' whilst out walking.

Common Ground has worked carefully and closely with both artists and local commissioners throughout the six commissions to date, in order to nurture and observe the early stages of the Project. The officer has had to adopt the role of 'commissions agent', in many ways similar to that offered by Regional Arts Associations or Public Art Agencies:

- promoting the idea of commissioning open air craftwork or
  sculpture.
- assisting with artist selection.
- liaising between artist and commissioner.

New Milestones

- creating new opportunities for permanent public art.
- advising on legal, planning and practical aspects.
- assisting with fundraising.

In addition to these tasks, the philosophy and aims of Common Ground and the New Milestones Project have provided further imperatives:

- working with local individuals or groups wanting to commission a work for the place where they live.
- actively seeking wider community involvement to discuss the theme and location for the work, to help fundraise, to give practical help and support to the artist and to join in celebrations and events.
- inviting genuine collaboration between artists and their local commissioners.
- encouraging local commissions which expand and highlight the enjoyment and familiarity which people find in their surroundings.

It is too early to say if the first six commissions have had any 'lateral' benefits to the community: If the commissions really have made people see their place in new and different ways; If communities have been brought closer together by the experience; If they see new opportunities to look after their places; If they envisage future collaborations with artists and craftspeople.

We are delighted with the ways in which the sculptors have interpreted their briefs and with the finished works. It is only with the last three commissions - at Godmanstone, Chiswell and Waterrow - that the community potential of the Project is being realised, with the help of a full time Project Officer, based in Dorset.

We have learned a multitude of lessons from the planning and execution of these New Milestones, many of which are referred to in the individual commission stories. Some however, are worth emphasising:

No two commissions are the same - this manual attempts to give helpful advice and warnings, but different problems will crop up to which new solutions can be found, and new excitements will appear.

Ownership - although the land in a locality may be legally owned by one major landholder, by the local authority or a patchwork of individuals and tenants, people who live in a place and are familiar with the roads, public paths and landscape have an emotional ownership of it. In a sense the land belongs to everyone. Heated emotions may be generated by plans to commission a sculpture, and the importance of local consultation cannot be overstressed: it will clarify intentions and calm fears, it helps engender understanding, support and personal commitment. It is quite feasible for local people to commission and own a sculpture to be placed on land which they do not own. It is, of course, necessary to have the permission and co-operation of the landholder, with whom a written agreement should be drawn up, covering ownership of the work, maintenance, accidental or wilful damage, insurance and the lifespan of the permission.

Matching the right community and artist is vital, creating the spark to lift an adequate, workmanlike piece of work to become a vibrant, living feature in a place. It is advisable to look at the work of artists beyond your area as well as those who live locally: a local artist may not do the job best simply because he/she knows the area well - an artist from outside may see anew what local people take for granted. The work will be permanent and will exist beyond the lives of present day inhabitants. Will it represent the best of our cultural aspirations and creativity? Time spent seriously exploring what the work will bring to the community - actual and emotional focus, identity, crystallisation, aspiration - repays the effort by helping to determine what qualities and interests to look for in an artist or craftsperson.

New Milestones

Thorough planning and preparation of a project, thinking through the various stages and spotting possible snags, will avoid problems and frustrations later. Detailed discussions between commissioner and artist, with written records of agreements, are essential to minimise misunderstandings and to develop a bond of trust and sympathy. The commissioning and creating of a permanent work is a pressured time for both parties. It is a working situation for the artist, exposed to public view, away from friends and family: for the commissioner, the project is an extra commitment beside work and everyday life. Tolerance, understanding and above all, time for regular frank discussions of progress and problems is needed from both sides.

The timescale of a commission can be lengthy - 18 months from first discussions to unveiling the work is average. Fundraising, local consultation, obtaining planning consent, and allowing adequate time (2 - 8 months) for the artist to develop a considered proposal can all be protracted. Fundraising in a rural situation where there are few businesses and little political muscle often requires reserves of conviction and tenacity.

Information plaques - None of the 'New Milestones' are labelled with date, title, or the names of sculptor, commissioners or funders. This has been at the suggestion of Common Ground, that passers-by might then see the work as surprise objects in the landscape, unfettered by notions of ART, and free of feelings of inadequacy or alienation. Information in leaflet or postcard form could be available locally. Our experience has been that this strategy has been largely successful with members of the public encouraging people to pause and speculate on the works. Some funding bodies and local councils have been keen to see an official plaque, but have agreed to alternative publicity through the local press, magazines, radio and television.

The commissioning of a 'New Milestone' will be time consuming, exhausting and frustrating for all concerned. It is also exciting, fun, optimistic and deeply rewarding to have a hand in creating a permanent statement of our culture for the future. Common Ground hopes that many more local groups nationwide will wish to celebrate their place with a permanent work of art or craft, taking courage from the enthusiasm, commitment, persistence and sheer hard work of those who have already taken part in the Project.

THE FUTURE

With the national launch of the New Milestones Project, Common Ground is assessing how best to encourage its extension to other parts of the country. It was never envisaged that it would be possible or desirable to place a New Milestones Officer in each county. Instead, it is hoped that the philosophy, approach and lessons of the pilot phase will be absorbed into the thinking and work of existing arts, environmental and community organisations, and that of local authorities.

The New Milestones Project has often been seen as a rural public art agency, similar to those working in mainly urban contexts.

New Milestones

The apparent rural emphasis has been because a largely rural county was chosen as the pilot area, but there is no reason why the same 'New Milestones' principles should not be applied and be successful in self-defining urban communities, neighbourhoods or groups of streets.

Common Ground has already begun exploring the Project's next stage in a northern and an eastern county. In Cleveland, with the support of Northern Arts, Common Ground has been collaborating with Steve Chettle, Visual Arts Officer with Cleveland Arts, the county's arts development organisation, to look for local commissioners and opportunities. Cleveland Arts has undertaken extensive local research and developed a wide network of new countryside, planning and local contacts. Common Ground has acted in an advisory capacity, making periodic visits to discuss progress, plan strategy and attend meetings. Two local authorities are already showing considerable interest: Hartlepool Borough Council's recently appointed Arts Development Officer has the New Milestones Project as a substantial area of work within his remit, and the Planning Department of Langbaurgh Borough Council is actively looking for opportunities in East Cleveland where New Milestones could be combined with reclamation work. Hilton Parish Council, with close support from Cleveland Arts, is preparing to commission 'markers' and / or a crossing for a stream.

In Lincolnshire, North Kesteven District Council has recently appointed a Rural Arts Worker, with promotion and support of New Milestones initiatives as a central part of the job description. Common Ground anticipates establishing a similarly warm collaboration here.

These two examples provide a model for Common Ground's future role in the development of the New Milestones Project. Stepping back from a close involvement with every commission, we hope to collaborate with regionally and locally based organisations, which are better placed geographically to give close support and help to local people. To these organisations we would wish to offer assistance in the areas of local consultation, conservation issues, selection of artists and discussion of locations and themes. We hope that a range of arts, environmental, community and statutory bodies will wish to adopt the promotion and support of New Milestones initiatives as part of their brief. In this way Common Ground hopes to launch the New Milestones Project nationally, so that local people in all parts of the country will be excited and enabled to take part in commissioning a work for the place in which they live.

PART II

COMMISSION INFORMATION AND CHECKLISTS

The information in this section is here to help you, not to scare you off! Remember that eating breakfast, learning to drive, growing lettuces, would all sound terribly complicated if you had to write them down.

It contains advice and checklists which are designed to assist you plan and manage a New Milestones commission. A bibliography and a list of organisations offering advice and help are included as sources of more up-to-date and detailed information than this book can encompass.

Do not be afraid to seek help when you need it and to find your own solutions to the challenges and problems you may encounter.

New Milestones

EXAMPLE TIMETABLE
MANOR FARM SCULPTURE

Aug 86 First letter from Common Ground to Will and Pam Best.
Dec 86 Initial meeting to discuss a sculpture at Manor Farm.
Jan 87 Discussion of themes, locations, costs. Meeting to shortlist sculptors . Draft budget drawn up. Commission brief sent to 4 sculptors.
Feb 87 Replies from artists; all interested. Final selection delayed in order to raise funds. Initial contact with potential funding bodies. Location for sculpture 'discovered'. Information sheet written.
Mar 87 Grant applications made to: S W Arts, TSW, Sir Edward Robinson Charitable Trust.
May 87 Selection of sculptor; Christine Angus chosen. Application responses: S W Arts £1,950, TSW £400
Jun 87 Initial 3 day visit by Christine Angus; discussions on theme, timetable, budget. 2nd visit by Christine with drawings of first ideas. Approved by the Bests, South West Arts and Common Ground.
Jul 87 Site meeting with District planning officer.
Aug 87 Christine visits Purbeck quarry to select stone. Approach to Cerne Valley Parish Council for support , £10 received. Donations of £800 from local people. Godmanstone Fete: display about the project. Article in Cerne Valley Parish Newsletter. Invitations to District and Parish Councillors to visit sculpture clearing and discuss project. Planning Application made. Grant application made to West Dorset District Council. First delivery of stone. Christine resolves form of sculpture, starts work in farmyard while planning consent awaited. Local leafletting. Picnic in sculpture clearing, £67 raised.Planning Permission granted.
Sep 87 West Dorset District Council grant - £100. British Organic Farmers annual weekend at Manor Farm.
Oct 87 Carving continues in farmyard.
Nov 87 Stones moved from farmyard to hilltop location. Neighbouring farmer plants daffodils in clearing.Donations from local people and passing walkers.
Dec 87 Meeting to review progress. Last phase postponed.
Mar 88 Christine returns to continue carving on site.
May 88 Sculpture completed.
Jun 88 Celebration picnic with local people, friends and funders.

CHOOSING AN ARTIST / CRAFTSPERSON

The aim of the New Milestones Project is to promote the idea of locally commissioned outdoor art and craft works which are an expression of our present day culture and environmental concerns and which deepen our understanding and appreciation of our local surroundings and countryside. The intention is that the works should have meaning for us today and continue to have vitality and presence in the future.

It is acceptable, indeed desirable, for a work of art to hold interwoven layers of meaning and reference: the artist's intentions, its personal meaning for the artist; different meanings for different viewers according to their interests and experiences; different meanings for the same person depending on mood, the weather, time of day or season.

Common Ground hopes that 'New Milestones' works will:

- deepen understanding of the locality
- draw on and highlight hidden aspects of the place
- express present day cultural and social aspirations
- respond to the particular place
- encourage pause and reflection
- generate discussion and stories
- create a greater sense of community
- be poetic and imaginative
- interest and intrigue people, now and in the future
- provoke active environmental and community care
- engender a sense of pride and 'ownership' by local people
- be aesthetically pleasing

Before looking at the work of possible artists/craftspeople. it is useful to devote at least one whole meeting to discussing the function or role the commissioned work will play in the community: eg. meeting place, focal point, landmark, quiet pausing point, waymark, aspiration, memory. This should help clarify and broaden ideas of what kind of work, materials, artist or craftsperson is needed.

Sculpture/Craft Slide Indexes

It is advisable to look at a slide index to see the range of work being made

New Milestones

and find new ideas. It may be possible to borrow slides of those artists/craftspeople you are particularly interested in to make your final selection at a local meeting.

The following organisations often have a slide index and may also assist with selecting the right artist for your place:
Regional Arts Association; Public Art Agency; Local Authority; County or District Arts Development Organisation; Crafts Council (the index is highly selective, but there is also a broader register of craftspeople); Common Ground.

Note
If the Regional Arts Association is to be approached for a grant, it will usually be a condition that the Visual Arts Officer or a panel member is involved in the selection process, agrees the choice of artist and approves the proposed work.

You will be choosing an artist/craftsperson on the evidence of their current and previous work, and asking them to make a new work which responds to your place and is for you and your community. You are therefore looking for qualities in the work and the artist which indicate that the commission stands the best chance of being a good experience for all parties and that it will result in the best possible piece of work. The following list of questions may be helpful:

The Artist
Is he/she: willing to welcome and listen to local discussion of the site and theme?
Sensitive to unspoken emotions behind the words?
Responsive to the resonances and hidden qualities of places?
Able to explain and discuss ideas and working methods?
Enthusiastic to work 'on site' or within the community, and to withstand adverse weather conditions.
Willing to use sensitive materials, and work with local materials and methods if appropriate?
Interested in the land and broader environmental concerns?

The Work
Do the artist's ideas excite interest, invite thought, provoke exploration?
Will the materials/techniques stand up to weather, accidental or wilful

damage?
How will it appear to people 25, 50, 100. 200 years hence?

An artist who has no interest in spending time in your place and with you should be avoided at the outset - the work he/she does may be terrific but it will be for him/her and of him/her, not for you and your place with him/her.

It may be helpful to draw up a shortlist of 4 - 5 artists/craftspeople and to send them the commission brief asking if they would be interested and available. Their replies and comments may be useful in guiding the final selection.

Having arrived at a decision, it is important to invite the artist to visit you and your place for 2/3 days at least 2 months before the planned start of the commission. During his/her stay you will be able to get to know him/her, and can discuss themes and locations, as well as practical details such as the fee, budget, timetable, help in kind and so on. The artist should be offered expenses and a fee for this visit.

Before the commission starts, the artist should be asked to produce drawings of the sculpture/s he/she is proposing to create. The proposal must be agreed by you and by funding bodies which have made a grant offer subject to their approval of the design (eg the Regional Arts Association). Ideas for work which seem flimsy or inappropriate should be examined rigorously, and if need be, rejected for other ideas - something which begins wrongly seldom gets better.

New Milestones

COMMISSION BRIEF

The brief is intended to give an artist/craftsperson information about the commission being offered, and is also a useful means of clarifying the thoughts and expectations of the commissioner.

It should include the following details:

The commissioner/s - Parish Council, local group, literary society, individual, with names and brief information on members if appropriate.

Why a work is being commissioned - eg. to mark a significant event, to celebrate a place, to highlight a local ecological issue, interest in sculpture in the countryside.

General description of the area - location in country/county, topography, nearby towns, villages, streams, rivers, woodland, agriculture, industries.

Possible locations for the work - places which could be considered or which are important in the area, OR

Description of chosen place - reasons for choice, surroundings, size, particular features, relation to footpaths/roads, practical problems eg access by vehicles.

Possible themes - ideas already discussed, eg. geology, local work and traditions, local history and legends, an event, a person, the natural history etc.

The commissioner may have a good idea for a theme which has local significance, but should avoid imagining how the artist might interpret it. The final choice of subject matter should be arrived at with the artist.

Materials - certain stones, wood or techniques may be local to the area - include details if the artist is being asked to consider using them.

The Fee - what it includes. Any other benefits offered - free/cheap accommodation, materials in kind, services in kind, fee and expenses for preparatory visit or design costs. Other budget figures which will be available to the artist for the project.

Timescale envisaged - preferred timetable and completion date. These may need to be adjusted to suit the artist's other commitments.

CONSULTATION, ADVICE AND HELP

Consultation, both formal and informal, about a proposed commission may be needed with a wide range of statutory and voluntary organisations and bodies, as well as people living locally. Although time consuming, it is an excellent way of involving people and introducing an idea gradually, thus giving a project the best chance of being accepted. Many of the organisations listed will be able to give advice and help to ease the progress of a commission from idea to reality. The checklist below gives some ideas:

District or Borough Planning Department - Is formal planning consent needed? The local Planning Department will be able to advise and, in any case, will like to be kept informed of projects in the area in order to answer any enquiries. Ask if other departments or people in the District or County Council should be consulted eg. Engineers, Transport and Highways, Footpaths etc

County Transport and Highways Department - If the sculpture is to be placed beside or near a road, formal permission is needed. Ask for advice on requirements for foundations, safety etc.

Parish Council - will wish to receive information on projects taking place within the Parish. Planning applications are usually sent to the relevant Parish Council for comments. If there is enthusiastic local support for a sculpture commission, the Parish Council may agree to allocate the 'free two pence' (product of a 2p rate) as a grant towards the project. A planning application by a Parish Council made on its own behalf or that of a local group will cost half the usual fee.

The Landholder - It is possible for a sculpture commissioned by, for example, a Parish Council to be placed on land owned by a farmer, without the landholder owning the work, accepting maintenance or insurance implications, or losing any rights of ownership over the land. A written agreement giving permission should be drawn up between the sculpture commissioner/owner and the landholder defining the rights and responsibilities of each party.

Regional Arts Association - will wish to be informed of commissions in its region and may be able to help with advice on selecting an artist,

New Milestones

fundraising, legal contracts, as well as possibly assisting with a grant.

Nature Conservancy Council - Is the chosen location for the sculpture a Site of Special Scientific Interest or of conservation interest generally? If so, what constraints does this place on the sculpture and its fixing/positioning? Could any creative habitat work be done?

County Archaeologist - Is the place part of or near to a Scheduled Ancient Monument? Are there any generalarchaeological or historical implications?

Rural Community Council/Council for Voluntary Service - may be able to offer support to a local commission with advice on fundraising, contacts etc.

Local Community Arts/Arts Development Officers - based with the County or District Council, or with an independent organisation. May be able to offer support, fundraising advice, help with events etc.

It may also be necessary or useful to contact some of the following organisations and bodies, for local information and research, encouragement and support, co-operation with associated tree planting or footpath clearance.
NB The list is not exclusive!

Countryside Commission Regional Office
National Trust Regional Office
Woodland Trust
Forestry Commission
County Naturalists or Wildlife Trust
Farming and Wildlife Advisory Group County Branch
Groundwork Trust local branch
Ramblers Association County Branch
Council for the Protection of Rural England County Branch
National Farmers Union County Branch
Regional Water Authority
County Council: Countryside Section, County Tree Planting Scheme, County Footpaths Officer, County Archivist
County or local museum and/or Art Gallery

LOCAL CONSULTATION

At some stage in the planning of a commission, a local meeting, exhibition or event will be vital in order to inform and involve people outside the committee or organising group. This should take place before the sculptor/craftsperson begins making the commissioned work, to allow people to contribute to the discussion on the location and theme for the work. Local knowledge is your most reliable guide to the best timing.

The aim is to draw in as many local people as possible to take an interest and maybe to contribute in practical ways to the project. Invitations can be issued by house-to-house leafletting, posters in local meeting places (village/church hall,shop, post office, pub), in the Parish newsletter, and by letter to local groups, clubs and organisations: Women's Institute, Youth Club, Guide, Brownie, Cub, Scout, Rover and Ranger Companies, Primary/Secondary School, Parochial Church Council, Civic Society, Local History Group, Literary Society, Over Sixties Club, Working Men's Club, Horticultural or Allotments Society etc.

New Milestones

ARTIST AND COMMISSIONER

By agreeing to collaborate on a commission, the artist and commissioner(s) are entering into a business arrangement whereby each accepts certain responsibilities and expects certain rewards. The basic agreement between them is expressed in the Commission Agreement and the Contract of Sale. As well as these two formal contracts, it is essential that the two parties discuss the whole project in detail to clarify exactly what each expects from the other and what each has agreed to do, to agree the budget, and to identify in advance potential problems which may have logistical or financial implications. Agreements and understandings should be confirmed in writing.

The Commissioner is offering a fee and commission costs to the artist to make a permanent work, and is responsible for raising this sum and any materials/assistance in kind as agreed. He/she should obtain such permissions as are necessary (planning consent, permission of the landholder etc) and arrange opportunities for local people to become involved in the project (meetings, events, leaflets etc).

The Artist is undertaking to make an original work and is responsible for proposing a sculpture which can be made within the timescale and budget as agreed. He/she is expected to undertake all practical arrangements for making and fixing the sculpture unless otherwise agreed with the commissioner. A self-employed artist will almost certainly have other commitments (teaching, exhibitions etc) which will intervene during the commission work period. Time off for meeting friends, recreation etc are also essential. Having agreed the completion date, the artist must be free to organise his/her hours of work to finish the work in the time available, but should keep the commissioner informed of his/her plans.

The Artist's Fee is payment for the artist's time and expertise. The fee covers thinking time. designing and making drawings and/or maquettes; consulting with the community; attending local and planning meetings as required; and making the work itself. If the artist is invited to make an initial visit a separate fee and travel expenses should be offered to cover this.

Commission costs - the costs of making the work, (materials, equipment, transport etc) may be added to the artist's fee and paid directly to him/

her. Alternatively the commissioner may pay the bills. Some of the commission costs may be provided 'in kind'. The artist should be told the total sum available and should be involved in how it is allocated in the budget.

The Budget - What sums, if any, have been allocated towards costs such as materials, transport of materials, siting costs, equipment hire? How are bills agreed and paid, and what happens if there is overspend?

Assistance and Materials in kind
* Free/low cost accommodation - Where and for how long? Is it suitable? Does it include food, heating/lighting, bed linen, laundry facilities? The artist is working away from home and under considerable pressure in a public situation. Separate accommodation with privacy to relax, draw, think, read, sleep, is usually most desirable. Invitations to supper, outings, etc are however, often welcome.
* Materials - What exactly is being offered and are they suitable for the artist's needs? Can the artist choose the materials he / she requires ? How and when will materials be made available and who pays for transport?
* Transport of Materials - What vehicle is available and who is offering it? Is it adequate for the job? Will it be able to reach the location for the sculpture? What notice should be given and to whom in order to be sure transport will available when needed? If the sculpture site is remote, how will tools and equipment be moved there, will they need to be transported everyday or can they be stored securely nearby?
* Tools/Equipment - Is the artist expected to provide all the tools and equipment needed for making the work (generator, grinder, power saw, drill, scaffolding and tarpaulin, lifting gear)? Can equipment be borrowed or is there money in the budget to pay for hiring it?
* Assistance/Labour - What help will be needed by the artist and when? How much notice is needed to galvanise help and who arranges it?

The Site - Does this present problems for transporting materials, a need for shelter which may have budgetary implications?

Publicity/local consultation - How will people living in the vicinity be informed and involved in the project? Local meetings, talks, slideshows, an exhibition, fundraising events? Will formal meetings with Planning Officers, the Parish Council and others be needed? Is the artist expected to attend some or all of these?

New Milestones

COMMISSION AGREEMENT AND CONTRACT OF SALE

The Commission Agreement and Contract of Sale are legally binding documents, signed by the artist and commissioner/s. It is important that both parties read the documents together, and discuss the completion date, the description of the sculpture and the fee. The samples given are basic models covering essential information on the rights and obligations of both parties. They can be expanded to include more detailed agreements if required. It is advisable to consult a solicitor to draw up the final draft - ask your Regional Arts Association for advice.

The New Milestones Project is aiming to encourage permanent outdoor works for particular localities. As the commissioner will therefore own the work on its completion, the Commission Agreement and the Contract of Sale are drawn up and considered together. The Commission Agreement is signed before work on the commission begins, the Contract of Sale when the work is complete and the artist formally hands it over to the commissioner.

COMMISSION AGREEMENT

This AGREEMENT is made the.............day of 19.....
between
NAME...(THE ARTIST) of
ADDRESS...
TELEPHONE..
and
NAME...(THE COMMISSIONER) of
ADDRESS...
TELEPHONE..
by which we agree as follows:

1. COMMISSION
The Artist agrees to complete on or about the........day of.......19...**(1)** unless circumstances beyond his/her control render this impossible, the following proposed work(s) of art ("The Works"):
DESCRIPTION**(2)**...
DIMENSIONS...
MATERIALS..

2. PAYMENTS

(a) In consideration for creating the Work(s) the Commissioner agrees to pay the Artist the sum of £........... (excluding VAT)(3) in the following instalments:

(1) One third upon signing this Agreement and
(2) one third when the Artist notifies the Commissioner that the Work(s) is/are two-thirds completed and
(3) one third when the Artist notifies the Commissioner that the Work(s) is/are completed.

For these purposes, the Artist shall notify the Commissioner in writing and shall permit him/her or his/her authorised agents, upon reasonable notice, to inspect the Work(s).

(b) Subject to Clause 6 of this Agreement, the Artist shall retain the title of the Work(s), and all rights therein, until payment of the final instalment.

3. ACCEPTANCE

It is understood that the Artist will use his/her aesthetic skill and judgement to create the Work(s), and that the Commissioner agrees to accept the completed Work(s) unless he/she can show that the Work(s) was/were not executed substantially in accordance with the description agreed by him/her under Clause 1 of this Agreement.

4. ACCESS

If the Work(s) is/are to be created on site, the Commissioner shall arrange for the Artist and his/her authorised agents to have access at all reasonable times to the site between the........day of......... 19.. and the........day of...........19..

5. SALE

Upon completion of the Work(s) both parties shall sign the Contract of Sale (a copy of which is attached hereto).

6. TERMINATION

The Commissioner may terminate this Agreement at any time upon giving written notice to the Artist, who shall be entitled to receive or retain payment for all work done in pursuance of this Agreement up to date of receiving such notice. In the event of termination, title to the

New Milestones

Work(s) and all rights therein, shall be retained by the Artist.

7. PROPER LAW

This Agreement shall be governed by the Law of England and Wales and may only be amended in writing by both parties.

8. ARBITRATION

Any dispute shall be referred to an arbitrator to be nominated by ....(4) in accordance with the provision of the Arbitration Act 1950 or any Statutory modification or re-enactment thereof for the time being in force.

SIGNED...(The Commissioner)
....(The Artist)

NOTES

(1) Allow enough slack in the timetable for unforeseen delays (non delivery of materials, weather, broken equipment, sculptor's elbow etc). If the stated date is overrun, a revised completion date may be agreed by an exchange of letters between commissioner and artist.

(2) Title, approximate dimensions, materials, brief description.

(3) The fee pays for the artist's time and skill in designing and making the work. Does it also include an element for materials, accommodation and other costs of making the sculpture or are these covered by other allocations in the budget?

(4) The Arbitrator must be independent of both artist and commissioner. Ask if the Director of the Regional Arts Association, the local Community Council or the regional Public Art Agency would be prepared to nominate a suitable person should the need arise.

ARTIST'S CONTRACT OF SALE

This Agreement dated the........day of............19... is between

NAME...(The Artist)
ADDRESS..
TELEPHONE..
and
NAME...(The Buyer)
ADDRESS..
TELEPHONE..

who has agreed to purchase

"The Works" (1):...
....

subject to the following terms and conditions:

1. Property in the Work(s) will pass to the Buyer on payment of the final invoice.
2. The Artist warrants that the Work(s) is/are original and that no replica of it/them has been/will be made by him/her.
3. Copyright is retained by the Artist and the Buyer agrees to acknowledge the Artist as creator of the Work(s) at all times.
4. The Buyer has inspected the sculpture on completion and agrees that the Work(s) is/are safely installed to his/her satisfaction.(2)
5. The Buyer will take reasonable care of the Work(s) and will not intentionally alter/damage/destroy it/them or permit others to do so.
6. The Buyer shall allow public access to the Work(s) at all reasonable times.(3)
7. The Work(s) shall remain in the position(s) in which they have been placed by the sculptor, unless it is unavoidable to move them.
8. All risk of damage, destruction or prejudice in any way whatsoever to the Work(s) shall pass to the Buyer and in the event of repair being necessary the Buyer shall give the Artist the option to conduct or supervise any restoration work or repairs on terms to be agreed.(4)
9. On signing this Agreement all liability for damage, destruction or injury to anybody or anything howsoever arising from the sculpture shall pass to the Buyer.(5)

New Milestones

10. The Buyer will not sell, lend or remove the sculpture without first notifying the Artist who will keep the Buyer informed of any changes of address and whose consent will not unreasonably be witheld.**(6)**
11. This Agreement shall be governed by the Law of England and Wales.

SIGNED..(The Artist)
....(The Buyer)

NOTES
(1) Title of work.
(2) When the contract is signed, the buyer becomes liable for damage to or caused by the sculpture, therefore the work should be thoroughly checked for stability, sound workmanship etc.
(3) Public access must also be agreed with the owner of the land, if different from the buyer of the sculpture, and written into the document giving the landholder's permission to place the work in his/her land.
(4) The buyer may repair temporarily the work to make it safe, but should consult the artist or ask him/her to carry out permanent repairs for which a fee should be paid.
(5) Public Liability Insurance is essential to cover claims for damages. It is often possible to add cover for the sculpture to an existing policy at little extra cost (eg a Parish Council's policy to cover swings, playing field, bus shelter, or a farm's policy to cover machinery, hayricks, farm workers, buildings etc.)
(6) As is shown by this clause and nos. 3, 5 and 7, the artist retains important rights in the work which protect his/her original intentions and the integrity of the work.

FORMAL PERMISSIONS

PLANNING PERMISSION

Consult your local planning authority as early as possible in the preparatory stages of a commission. The Planning Officers can be supportive allies and are a valuable source of information and advice on the need for formal planning consent, how to make an application, where to ask if other permissions are required, useful contacts. They are as concerned as you are about maintaining the integrity of the place and the enthusiasm of local people.

The legislation drawn up to guide local authorities in planning decisions was not devised with the permanent placing of outdoor sculptures in mind. It is therefore open to some interpretation by individual planning officers and committees.

The two relevant Acts are the Town and Country Planning Act 1971 and the Town and Country Planning General Development Order 1971 which have been subject to recent amendments which considerably relax planning control. Check with your local Planning Officer about new amendments which may affect your application. These Acts are principally designed to govern housing and industrial development of land, extensions to dwellings, changes in land use (eg from agriculture to a BMX track), extraction of minerals and so on. Works of art will be generally be regarded as 'development' or 'change of use'. Some works may be exempt from the need for formal planning approval because of their form, (eg gates, walls or fences below a certain height), or because they are to be placed 'within the curtilage of a dwelling house' (ie domestic grounds).

Planning law is not primarily intended to arbitrate on the aesthetics of a work of art or craft. However the Committee will inevitably be influenced by the appearance of the work and its relationship to the proposed site, as well as by evidence of local support for the proposal. The Planning Officer should be interested to make sure you respect rights of way, archaeological or nature conservation sites and so on.

New Milestones

Making an Application

Forms and notes for the guidance of applicants are available from your local Planning Office and you will be given help in completing the form if you need it. If the applicant is not the owner of the land where the sculpture is to be sited, a formal notice must be served on the owner and Certificate B must be completed, available from the Planning Office.

With the completed form, you will need to include:

- A general map of the area showing the position of the site.
- A site plan of 1:2500 scale or larger.
- A full description of the work: dimensions, materials, siting etc.
- Clear drawings/diagrams of the proposed work in relation to the location. These may need to be specially made by the artist.
- Details of theme, reasons for commissioning, choice of location, local support etc.
- Information on the artist/craftsperson: Curriculum Vitae, details of other public commissions undertaken, photos of previous work.

A fee is payable and must be included with the application. If the applicant is a Parish Council, the fee is halved.

Notes
* Allow adequate time for the application to be processed - it can take up to two months, or more if the Committee requests further information.
* Invite the Planning Officer for a discussion at the proposed sculpture site before making the application.
* Seek the support of your Parish Council. The District Council will usually ask for the Parish Council's views on applications in their Parish.
* Invite individual Parish Council and District Council Planning Committee members to visit the site and discuss the project.
* Ensure that your local District councillor on the Planning Committee is fully informed and supportive.

OTHER CONSENTS

Public Highways - If the location of the work is near a public highway, permission from the County Highways, Transport or Engineering Department may be required. Seek advice from the relevant officer.

Ancient Monument - Consult the County Archaeologist to find out if the proposed location is a Scheduled Ancient Monument. If so, you will need to seek Scheduled Monument Consent, or better, find another place, to avoid disturbing archaeological remains.

Site of Special Scientific Interest or nature reserve of any kind - The owner of the land should know if the proposed location is within an SSSI. If so, you will need to consult the local office of the Nature Conservancy Council. In general any work which will disturb the soil or involve damage to flora or fauna will not be acceptable and the NCC will oppose planning consent.

Conservation Area or Listed Buildings - consult the Planning Officer and Architect's Department about designations in your locality.

Public Utilities - If the chosen location for the commissioned work is near to housing or industry, digging foundations may disturb gas, water, sewerage pipes, electricity mains or underground telephone cables. It is therefore advisable to consult the individual authorities or the County Council to check the location of mains services.

New Milestones

FUNDRAISING

There will almost always be a need to raise quite substantial sums of money, and probably donations of help or materials in kind for a locally based commission to go ahead. The process can be lengthy, needing to coincide with 6 weekly or 3 monthly committee cycles, and can be fraught with anxiety if responses are slow arriving or requests for funds are turned down. TAKE HEART. Others have managed to raise the necessary funds, with optimism and persistence, and you can do the same. Given good local support for the idea, a well thought out proposal, the right artist for the right place, thorough planning and research, conviction and determination, it can be done.

There may be local or regional organisations which can give advice and help with fundraising, drawing up a budget and applications:

Regional Arts Association - Visual Arts, Crafts, Community Arts or Sponsorship officer.
Public Art Agency - some RAAs have devolved responsibility for Public Art commissioning to independent agencies. Check with your RAA. These bodies have to draw some of their income from their 'clients' and may make a charge for their advice or assistance. This cost can be included in the commission budget.
County, District or Borough Council - Arts Development Officer, Community Leisure Officer.
Rural Community Council - Fieldworker, Rural Arts Officer, Rural Development Area worker.
Local Arts Development Organisation
Community Arts Organisation

Notes
* Allow adequate time for fundraising - 3 months at the very least, 6 months or more is realistic.
* Contact potential sources of funding by telephone or letter before submitting a formal application. Find out their policy guidelines, dates of meetings, latest submission dates, the level of request to make.
* Direct your applications to funding bodies which include art, environmental care and improvement or community projects as part of their policy. Careful individual applications are more effective than duplicated mass appeals.

* If the Regional Arts Association is to be approached the officer will usually wish to be consulted at a very early stage on artist selection, before the choice is made.

* Funders like to be one of a spectrum of funding bodies - aim for a mixture of public, business and local grants and donations.

* Assistance or materials given in kind or at cost price should be included against income and expenditure in your budget, valued at the commercial rate you would otherwise have paid. This is essential as many organisations will only give a percentage figure of the total budget so your figures should reflect in pounds sterling all the support you are receiving in other forms.

* Many Trusts and Foundations will only give grants to charities, not to individuals or local groups. The Village Hall committee, Residents' Association or other organisations in your area may be registered as a charity. Ask if they would be prepared to put forward an application and receive the money on your behalf - it is a good way of getting them involved.

* Evidence of local support is important to convince some funding sources. The range of organisations on the committee, the support of the Parish Council or Residents Association etc, (verbally and with a donation), local people involved in fundraising events, giving materials, help or time towards the project, are all persuasive factors.

* Local Fundraising is an important element - not only does it show that local people really support the idea, but it will actually increase commitment locally.

SOURCES

Regional Arts Association - Art in Public Places or Local Initiatives budget, or Public Art Agency

County, District or Borough Council - Community Leisure Department, Art and Recreation Department, Planning Department, Tourism Department.

Parish Council (see note)

Local Businesses - Industry, national stores, banks, breweries, television and radio stations, local family businesses, pubs.

Locally based trusts - see The Directory of Grant Making Trusts, published by the Charities Aid Foundation, in your local reference library.

Local donations - cash or kind

Local Fundraising - jumble sales, car boot or suitcase sales, auctions, coffee mornings, stall at fete or local market, village garden open day, raffle, social events (eg picnic, barn dance, concert), sponsored events, advertising and charging for bluebell walks, cross country riding on special occasions.

NOTE: Parish Councils and the 'Free Two Pence'

Financial support from your Parish or Town Council will generally be modest and will be a donation from current resources. However, you may be able to persuade them to give you a larger grant by using their ability to acquire additional funds for particular projects under their 'free two pence' power.

All Parish Councils (under section 137 of the Local Government Act 1972) are able to spend up to the product of a 2p rate, subject to a few limitations, on anything which is considered by the council to be 'in the interests of their area or any part of it, or all or some of its inhabitants'. This is known as the 'free two pence'. The power is commonly used by parish councils for such things as village improvements, litter clearing, tree planting; grants or donations to local voluntary organisations, youth clubs, village hall committees; or for local entertainments, local festivals etc. Depending on the penny rate product of your parish, the amount of money available under this power may amount to a few hundred or even several thousand pounds. The parish council raises this money from the local community through its annual rate precept on the District or Borough Council.

See also Holding Your Ground (Chapter 17, Money and Help), by Angela King and Sue Clifford (Wildwood House, 1987)

CHECKLIST 1
GRANT APPLICATION

An application should be concise, (up to two A4 pages), and should cover the following points:

The Commissioner/s
Name, address, telephone number, name of person to contact. Names of committee members and organisations (if relevant). Background information - how the group was formed; when discussions on the project began; who the commissioners are (Parish Council, specially formed group, farmers, etc), other bodies advising (eg Community Council).

The Project
How the decision to commission a sculpture came about.
Reasons for commissioning.
Aims of the project.

The Place
General description of the area.
Map and description of the chosen place for the sculpture, including its size, location, surroundings, public access.
Reasons for choosing this particular spot.

The Artist
Curriculum Vitae and photographs/slides of previous work.
Why selected for this project.

The Proposal
Drawings, photographs of maquettes, models etc for this project. Description of the proposal, subject, materials to be used. Why relevant to the locality.

The Timetable
Including starting date, planned events, anticipated completion date.

Local Consultation and Publicity
Details of plans to involve and inform local people including:
local meetings, talks, events, exhibitions, fundraising activities, leaflet production and distribution, plans to attract press coverage, unveiling party.

Finance
Budget sheet including anticipated expenditure and income (see budget checklist).
How the finances will be managed and by whom.

Amount requested

CHECKLIST 2
BUDGET

The breakdown of possible costs under each main heading is intended to help you draw up a realistic budget with the artist without missing out vital and expensive items. Funding organisations do not generally want to see this amount of detail, so for grant applications use only the main headings with the total for each group of costs. Remember to give figures for total expenditure and total anticipated income.

EXPENDITURE
Artist's Fees
  Artist's Commission Fee
  Preparatory visit by artist - fee for two days + travel expenses.
Materials and equipment
  Materials - eg. stone, wood, metal, etc
  Additional materials - eg. bolts, fixings, preservatives, stains.
  Transport of materials - eg. low loader with crane, truck.
  Equipment required by artist - eg. scaffolding, generator, winch
Other commission costs
  Assistance required by artist - eg. labour, specialist skills.
  Siting of work - eg. transport, crane, foundations, hole digging, fixing.
  Planning permission
  Insurance - public liability   Insurance for volunteers
Accommodation
  Accommodation for artist
Administration
  Basic Administration - Photocopying, postage, stationery, report
  Leaflet production - for distribution to community
  Publicity - press releases, photography.
  Unveiling/launch costs - eg. hospitality to funders and helpers.
Contingency - 10% of budget total.

INCOME
Contribution from commissioner - value of cash and help in kind
Grant offers - name of organisation and amount.
Applications under consideration - Name of organisation and grant requested.
Local fundraising - target amount.
Other local assistance - cash value of services/help offered.

USEFUL ADDRESSES

NOTE: See Common Ground's book, **Holding Your Ground - an action guide to local conservation**, by Angela King and Sue Clifford (Wildwood House, 1987) for a comprehensive list of addresses for environmental, community and art organisations.

STATUTORY

Arts Council of Great Britain, 105 Piccadilly, London W1V 0AU (01 629 9495) (for addresses of English Regional Arts Associations)
Countryside Commission, John Dower House, Crescent Place, Cheltenham, Glos. GL50 3RA (0242 521381)
Countryside Commission for Scotland, Battleby, Redgerton, Perth PH1 3EW (0738 27921)
Countryside Commission for Wales, 8 Broad Street, Newtown, Powys SY16 2LU (0686 26799)
Crafts Council, 12 Waterloo Place, London SW1Y 4AU (01 930 4811)
English Heritage, Fortress House, 23 Savile Row, London W1X 1AB (01 734 6010)
Forestry Commission, 231 Corstorphine Road, Edinburgh EH12 7AT (031 334 0303)
Nature Conservancy Council, Northminster House, Northminster, Peterborough, Cambs PE1 1UA (0733 40345).
Nature Conservancy Council (Scotland), 12 Hope Terrace, Edinburgh EH9 2AS (031 447 4784)
Nature Conservancy Council (Wales), Plas Penrhos, Penrhos Road, Bangor, Gwynedd LL57 2LQ (0248 55141)
Scottish Arts Council, 19 Charlotte Square, Edinburgh EH2 4DF (031 226 6051) (for addresses of Scottish Regional Arts Associations)
Welsh Arts Council, Museum Place, Cardiff CF1 3NX (0222 394711) (for addresses of Welsh Regional Arts Associations)

VOLUNTARY

ACRE, Stable Yard, Fairford Park, Fairford, Glos GL7 4JQ (0285 713210) (national body for Rural Community Councils)
Association for the Protection of Rural Scotland, 1 Thistle Court, Edinburgh 2 (031 225 6744)
Civic Trust, 17 Carlton House Terrace, London SW1Y 5AW (01 930 0914)
Civic Trust for Wales, St Michael's College, Llandaff, Cardiff CF5 2YJ (0222 552388)

New Milestones

Council for the Protection of Rural England (CPRE), 4 Hobart Place, London SW1W 0HY (01 235 9481)

Council for the Protection of Rural Wales, Ty Gwyn, 31 High Street, Welshpool. Powys SY21 7PJ (0938 2525) (see APRS for Scotland)

Country Landowners Association, 16 Belgrave Square, London SW1X 8PQ (01 235 0511)

Farming and Wildlife Advisory Group (FWAG), The Lodge, Sandy, Bedfordshire SG19 2DL (0767 80551)

Groundwork Foundation, Bennett's Court, 6 Bennett's Hill, Birmingham, B2 5ST (021 236 8565) For addresses of local Groundwork Trusts.

National Association of Local Councils, 108 Great Russell Street, London WC1B 3LD (01 636 4066) For information, training, etc

National Council for Voluntary Organisations, 26 Bedford Square, London SW1X 7NJ (01 636 4066)

National Farmers Union, Agriculture House, Knightsbridge, London SW1 7NJ (01 235 5077)

National Federation of Women's Institutes, 39 Eccleston Street, London SW1W 9NT (01 730 7212)

Ramblers Association, 1/5 Wandsworth Road, London SW8 2LJ (01 582 6878)

Royal Society for Nature Conservation (RSNC), The Green, Nettleham, Lincoln LN2 2NR (0522 752326) (for addresses of County Trusts for Nature Conservation)

Scottish Civic Trust, 24 St George Square, Glasgow G2 1EF (041 221 1466)

The Woodland Trust, Autumn Park, Dysart Road, Grantham, Lincolnshire NG31 6LL (0476 74297)

SELECT BIBLIOGRAPHY

A Sense Of Place: Sculpture in Landscape, eds. Peter Davies and Tony Knipe, (Ceolfrith Press, 1984)

Art Beyond the Gallery in early 20th century England, Richard Cork (Yale University Press, Newhaven and London, 1985)

Art for Architecture, ed. Deanna Petherbridge (HMSO, 1987)

Art Within Reach, ed. Peter Townsend (Art Monthly/Thames and Hudson, 1984)

Collected Artlaw Articles, Henry Lydiate, ed. Jenny Boswell (Artlaw Services, 1981)

Dorset, Christopher Taylor (The Making of the English Landscape County Volumes, Hodder and Stoughton, 1970)

Earthworks and Beyond: Contemporary Art in the Landscape, John Beardsley (Abbeville Press, New York, 1984)

Historic Landscape of Weld - The Weld Estate, Dorset, eds. Laurence Keen and Ann Carreck (Lulworth Heritage Ltd, c/o The Weld Estate, Lulworth Castle, East Lulworth, Dorset, 1987)

Holding Your Ground - An action guide to local conservation, Angela King and Sue Clifford (Wildwood House, 1987)

Living with the Past - the Historic Environment, D Baker (Bedford, 1983)

Making Ways, ed. David Butler (Artic Producers, 1987)

Open Air Sculpture, W J Strachan (Zwemmer/Tate Gallery, 1984; new edition imminent)

Parish Maps, Tom Greeves (Common Ground, 1987)

Peakland Roads and Trackways, A E Dodd and E M Dodd, (Moorland Publishing Company, 1974)

Powers and Constitution of Local Councils, Charles Arnold Baker, revised John Clark (National Association of Local Councils, 1979)

Roads and Tracks of Britain, Christopher Taylor (Dent, 1979)

Second Nature, eds. Richard Mabey, Susan Clifford and Angela King (Cape, 1984)

Sources of Funding for Countryside Projects, Sarah Buchanan, (The Volunteer Centre, 29 Kings Road, Berkhamsted, Herts.)

The Archaeology of Rural Dorset, L M Groube and M C B Bowden (Dorset Natural History and Archaeological Society, Monograph 4, 1982)

The Common Ground, Richard Mabey (Hutchinson, 1980)

The Countryside We Want - A Manifesto for the Year 2000, eds. Charlie Pye Smith and Chris Hall (Green Books, 1987)

New Milestones

The Directory of Grant Making Trusts, (Charities Aid Foundation, 48 Pembury Road, Tonbridge, Kent)

The Dorset Coast - a Geological Guide, G M Davies (Adam and Charles Black, 1935, 1970)

The Drovers, K J Bonser (Macmillan, 1970)

The Fields Beneath, Gillian Tindall (Temple Smith, 1977; Granada 1980)

The History of the Countryside, Oliver Rackham (Dent, 1986)

The Lost Roads of Wessex, C Cochrane (Augustus M Kelly, 1969)

The Making of the English Landscape, W G Hoskins (Penguin, 1985)

The Old Roads of Dorset, Ronald Good (Longmans, 1940; Horace G Commin Ltd, Bournemouth, 1966)

The Parish Boundary, Tom Greeves (Common Ground, 1987)

The Secret Country, Janet and Colin Bord (Granada, 1976)

White Horses and Other Hill Figures, Morris Marples (Alan Sutton, 1981)